The Lost Map To Your Career

A Practical Career Self Help Book for Navigating and Overcoming Self-Imposed Limits

Published by: Shyam Uthaman

Shyam Uthaman

Copyright © 2025. All rights reserved.

No part of this book may be reproduced, distributed, or transmitted in any form or by any means, including photocopying, recording, or other electronic or mechanical methods, without the prior written permission of the publisher, except in the case of brief quotations embodied in critical reviews and certain other noncommercial uses permitted by copyright law. For permission requests, please contact the publisher.

Disclaimer:

The views and opinions in this book are based on the author's personal experiences and insights and do not reflect the views of current or prior employers. While every effort has been made to ensure accuracy, this book is intended as general guidance, not a definitive source for career advice.

The publisher and author are not responsible for errors, omissions, or inaccuracies. Humor and anecdotes are included to engage and educate, not to offend. Examples and characters are fictionalized or anonymized, with any resemblance to real people being coincidental.

Results will vary, and no guarantees are made. Readers should seek professional advice for their unique situations. This book aims to inspire learning, growth, and empowerment.

Table of Contents:

Introduction: The Invisible Ceiling 5
Foundational Wisdom 10
   The Corporate Maze – Building Networks That Matter 11
   Prioritizing in a World of Chaos 20
   Communication and Transparency 29
   Navigating Corporate Politics without Losing Yourself 40
Self-Mastery and Personal Growth 49
   Learning from Mistakes – Growth Through Failure 50
   Reinventing Yourself – Sailing Where the Wind Blows 59
   Overcoming Impostor Syndrome and Self-Doubt 66
   Building Resilience and Maintaining Sanity 74
   Getting Out of Your Own Way 81
Mastering Relationships and Influence 87
   Becoming a Leader Before the Title 88
   The Art of Self-Promotion Without Bragging 97
   Creating Your Personal Brand 105
   Voicing Concerns and Tackling Conflict 115
   Asking for Help – Leveraging Your Network 124
   Finding Mentors and Becoming One 133
   Building Influence in a Remote/Hybrid World 143
Adapting to Change and Embracing Fear 154
   Fear and Freedom 155
   Managing Burnout and Knowing When to Step Back 166
   Handling the Unexpected 177

Trusting Your Instincts 188
The Long Game and Final Wisdom 198
The Power of Asking Why 199
Mastering Office Diplomacy 212
The Importance of Celebrating Wins—Big and Small 224
Sustaining Career Growth Over Time 234
Conclusion – Tying It All Together 245

Introduction: The Invisible Ceiling

Ever feel like you're trapped on a treadmill, running at full speed but getting nowhere? Do you feel like work is a popularity contest, and despite pouring your heart into every project, you're still overlooked while others seem to glide ahead?

Yeah, I've been there too. Like many of us, I used to believe that hard work alone was the secret to success. "Just keep grinding and everything will work out," they said. But over the years, I realized that wasn't enough. Success isn't just about hard work; it's about visibility, relationships, and playing the game—a game no one tells you the rules for.

It's frustrating to see someone like Chad—you know the type, effortlessly charming and always in the right rooms—get ahead while you're left wondering, "What am I missing?" The truth hit me like a ton of bricks: the work doesn't speak for itself. Corporate life isn't a meritocracy; it's a maze. To succeed, you need more than skill—you need strategy.

Why I'm Writing This Book

Here's the thing: I wasn't always good at navigating this maze. In fact, I made every mistake in the book. I played it safe when I should've spoken up, avoided conflict instead of addressing it, and believed good work would naturally lead to recognition. I doubled down on effort, assuming sheer willpower would open doors—but it didn't. Through trial, error, and a few humbling moments, I learned to rewrite the rules for myself, a process that revealed what I call the "invisible ceiling." This barrier—built of unspoken rules, quiet alliances, and unconscious biases—can stall your progress without you even realizing why. Recognizing it isn't about cheating the system; it's about finally seeing it clearly so you can chart your own path.

This book isn't about shortcuts or tricks. It's about helping you build real skills—the kind that make your efforts count. Along the way, I'll share lessons from both my failures and successes, showing you how to approach challenges with confidence and integrity. Whether it's mastering office politics, building a personal brand that opens doors, or learning to adapt when the rules keep shifting, you'll gain practical tools to shape your own success story. More importantly, you'll see that success isn't just about climbing any ladder—it's about picking the right one. In a world where everyone is working hard, the real differentiator lies in making your impact visible to those who hold the keys to your next opportunity. By the end, you'll understand not only how to show your value but how to position it in ways that truly matter.

I also realized that visibility and relationships were just as important as competence. In many workplaces, your reputation precedes you. If you're not actively shaping that narrative, someone else might be doing it for you—or no one at all. This book aims to demystify those hidden currents and give you the clarity and confidence to navigate them effectively.

Perspective and Relevance

In today's environment, success also hinges on how you respond to shifting demands. You need this if you're job hunting, just starting your job, or already working. You could excel in your role yet remain invisible if you aren't plugged into the bigger corporate narrative. By expanding your perspective—understanding not just what you do, but how it aligns with the organization's goals—you become more than a mere cog in the machine. You become someone whose contributions have depth and direction. This awareness is part of what sets top performers apart from those who stay stuck under the radar.

What This Book Will Do for You

By the time you finish, you'll know how to:
- Build a network that accelerates your career, not just your LinkedIn connections.
- Communicate with clarity and confidence, even when delivering bad news.
- Navigate office politics without selling your soul.
- Turn failures into stepping stones for growth.

We'll dive into real stories and actionable strategies to help you tackle the challenges you're likely facing—feeling invisible despite your hard work, struggling to balance priorities, or wondering how to stay relevant in a rapidly changing workplace. You'll learn to align your goals with your organization's needs while staying true to yourself. This book isn't just about career tips; it's about empowerment, giving you the confidence to take ownership of your journey.

And because I know every career path comes with its own set of unique challenges, I've put together a free Career FAQ eBook answering some of the most common and pressing career questions with everything from handling difficult bosses to accelerating your promotions. You can grab your copy here: www.shyamuthaman.com/careerFAQs. It's my way of giving you an extra tool to navigate your career with confidence.

The Maze No One Told You About

The corporate world isn't built for those who sit back and wait. It rewards people who understand how to position themselves, build meaningful relationships, and align their goals with the organization's. It's about knowing how to make yourself indispensable.

In the chapters ahead, we'll explore how to master these skills. We'll talk about building influence before you have a title, tackling impostor syndrome, and leveraging failures as opportunities. You'll learn to adapt to change, advocate for yourself, and create opportunities where none seem to exist.

This book is here to help you understand the game and give you the tools to play it your way. And yes, we'll find humor in the absurdities along the way—because if you can't laugh at the chaos, what's the point?

Let's get started on this journey of self-realization.

Section 1

Foundational Wisdom

Chapter 1

The Corporate Maze – Building Networks That Matter

Are you someone who believes that hard work alone will get you to the top? If you are, you're not alone—I used to think that too. I wore my work ethic like a badge of honor, convinced that clocking extra hours would naturally lead to success. But then, after years of watching colleagues like Chad breeze through promotions, I realized that while hard work is necessary, it's far from sufficient. It's like trying to win a race while ignoring the map—you might be fast, but are you heading in the right direction? Let me save you a decade of mistakes and late realization. Read on...

The Upward Network: Who's Pulling You Up?

In every organization, certain people have the power to influence your career trajectory—whether they're officially your boss or not. These are the ones who hold sway in decision-making, and aligning yourself with them can be a game changer. But let's get one thing straight: building an upward network isn't about sucking up. It's about creating authentic relationships where mutual benefit exists.

Take Chad, for instance. He had a knack for getting into the right rooms and chatting with the right people. While I was head-down in work, he was casually chatting up leadership in the break room, forming relationships that would later pay off. I used to scoff, thinking he was wasting time, but then I noticed how his ideas were getting traction. At first, I thought it was just schmoozing. But then I realized that Chad wasn't being insincere; he was just better at seeing the value of connecting with those who could help him grow. He once mentioned that "networking isn't about collecting new contacts; it's about being intentionally present so you become top-of-mind for the right people." That small shift in perspective transformed my view of networking from a self-serving tactic into a genuine leadership skill.

The lesson I learned? It's not about trying to be Chad, but rather understanding what he got right—building an upward network of people who believed in him, who thought of him when new opportunities arose. So, instead of grumbling about it, I decided to be more strategic about my own relationships.

I started asking myself: "Who are the key people in my organization? Who do I want to build a relationship with?" I made a list and began finding ways to interact with them—volunteering for projects they were involved in or simply striking up conversations about shared interests. I made an effort to offer my help on their projects, to be the person they could trust for accurate information and timely solutions. Over time, it paid off. Those relationships helped me gain visibility and access to opportunities I wouldn't have had otherwise.

The Downward Network: Who's Got Your Back?

While an upward network is crucial, your peers and those who report to you are just as important. This is your "downward network," and it's not just about getting things done—it's about building loyalty and trust.

I learned this the hard way. There was a time when I took on a large, complex project, thinking leadership would be impressed if I pulled it off solo. In reality, they weren't. And I was left burnt out and frustrated because I'd tried to do it all myself.

What I missed was that I had a team who could have helped me, and peers who were eager to contribute. But I hadn't built those relationships, so I ended up carrying the weight alone. I remember staring at a mountain of work one night, realizing there was no way I'd meet the deadline. That's when it hit me—I didn't have to do it all myself. Now, I see things differently. I make a point to support my team, to mentor those who need guidance, and to be a sounding board for my peers.

Your downward network isn't just there to help you—they're there to help you succeed as a team. If you show up for them, they'll show up for you when it counts. When you pull people up, you build a foundation of trust that can support you during tough times.

Generosity Is the Secret Sauce

Networking isn't about using people. It's about generosity. The best networks are built on a foundation of trust and reciprocity. Your upward network helps you because they know you provide value, and your downward network supports you because they know you have their back.

Chad, despite all the teasing, understood this well. His relationships weren't transactional; he built genuine connections by being helpful and showing up when it mattered. So, instead of envying Chad, I started thinking about how I could build relationships based on what I could give, not just what I could get.

I began volunteering for cross-functional teams, not just to gain visibility but to genuinely contribute. I offered my skills where they were needed without immediately thinking about how it would benefit me. And guess what? People noticed—not just the higher-ups but my peers, too. Opportunities started coming my way, not because I was seeking them out but because others thought of me when they arose.

Building Bridges, Not Walls

Here's the truth—visibility matters. You can be the hardest worker in the room, but if no one knows who you are, your efforts might go unnoticed. I stopped viewing networking as "political maneuvering" and started seeing it as an essential part of leadership and growth. It's not just about getting ahead—it's about lifting others as you go.

I began making my work visible in a way that wasn't boastful. I set up regular one-on-one meetings with key stakeholders—not just my boss, but those who interacted with my work. I shared updates, asked for feedback, and found out what challenges they were facing and how I could help. It wasn't just about sharing my achievements; it was about creating a two-way dialogue.

The more I communicated, the more opportunities opened up. I was no longer just a name on an email chain—I was someone they thought of when new projects came around. It felt like stepping out of the shadows into the light; suddenly, my contributions were part of the larger narrative. That's the power of visibility: making sure that the right people know what you're working on and how you can help them succeed too.

The Takeaway

Networking is not just about rubbing elbows with the right people; it's about forming authentic, mutually beneficial relationships that can shape your career. It's a long-term investment, where giving is just as important as receiving. By actively building and nurturing your upward, peer, and downward networks, you're laying a foundation for growth, resilience, and influence. Remember, a network built on genuine connections is like a safety net—you might not need it every day, but it's invaluable when you do. And remember, your network is only as strong as the trust and value you bring to it.

Action Plan: Building Networks That Matter

Objective: Build a strong network by forming authentic, mutually beneficial relationships with key individuals who can support your growth and success.

Framework: Use the following steps to build intentional relationships with upward, peer, and downward networks, creating a foundation for career growth and influence.

1. Identify Key People Quickly

Choose three influential people in your area by observing who drives discussions in meetings.

Example: Schedule a 15-minute chat with one of them to introduce yourself or discuss a shared project. This helps you establish visibility and rapport early on.

2. Set a Goal for Upward Networking

Select a high-impact project and plan to share an update with stakeholders this week, focusing on how your work aligns with team or department goals.

Example: If you're working on a strategic initiative, share a brief update that highlights its value to the organization, like increased efficiency or cost savings.

3. Maintain Regular Check-ins with Your Upward Network

o **Monthly**: Keep immediate decision-makers informed of your progress.

o **Quarterly**: Connect with those who influence promotion discussions.

o **Biannually**: Reach out to senior leaders in your extended network who impact your field.

Example: Send a quarterly email to update your manager on key achievements or request feedback. For senior leaders, a brief check-in every six months can keep you on their radar.

4. Prepare an Elevator Pitch

Draft a concise summary of your role, goals, and alignment with the company's mission for impactful introductions.

Example: "Hi, I'm [Your Name]. I focus on streamlining our team's operations to improve efficiency. My current project on [Project Name] has reduced our processing time by 20%, aligning with our goal to drive productivity."

5. Build Loyalty with Your Peers

Networking isn't just about upward connections; building trust among peers is essential

Example: Offer help to a peer who could use support, such as by giving feedback on their project or collaborating on a task. Showing you care about their success fosters mutual support.

6. Share Wins by Celebrating Team Successes

Increase visibility in a genuine way by highlighting team achievements and giving credit where it's due.

Example: In your next team meeting, recognize a recent team win and acknowledge each member's contribution. This approach builds goodwill and demonstrates appreciation for others.

Reflection and Self-Monitoring

Weekly Reflection: "What new connection or interaction did I make this week, and what was its value?"

Monthly Reflection: Reflect on the strength of your relationships within your upward, peer, and downward networks. Identify one action to deepen a specific relationship in the coming month.

Chapter 2

Prioritizing in a World of Chaos

Thursday afternoons always felt like a chaotic whirlwind. Three deadlines loomed over me like dark clouds, my next meeting was in five minutes, and Chad had just posted an Instagram story of himself at a rooftop bar. Meanwhile, I was staring at my screen, wondering how it was possible that he managed to have time for lunch breaks while I couldn't even fit in a coffee.

It took me longer than I'd like to admit to figure out Chad's secret. He wasn't doing less work; he just wasn't trying to do everything at once. That's when it clicked: getting ahead wasn't about doing more—it was about doing the right things in the right order.

We've all been there: the never-ending to-do list, the surprise project that lands in your lap, and the relentless stream of meetings that seem to multiply out of thin air. It's chaos, and for a long time, I thought the only way to survive was to work harder—stay later, get up earlier, power through. But all that led to was burnout and frustration.

What I didn't realize then is that it wasn't about doing more work—it was about doing the right work, at the right time.

The Art of Prioritization

One of the most important lessons I learned in my career is that not all tasks are created equal. Some tasks are like screaming toddlers demanding attention, others are quiet and truly important, and some are just distractions in disguise. If you don't learn to differentiate between them, you'll find yourself working endlessly without making meaningful progress.

Take that Thursday afternoon I mentioned earlier. I had three big projects on my plate, each with tight deadlines. My instinct was to try and tackle them all at once, jumping from one to the next like a ping-pong ball, hoping I could keep everything afloat. Within hours, it was clear this strategy was a disaster. Nothing was moving forward, and I was losing my grip.

Here's where I learned the value of the Minimum Viable Product (MVP) approach—and this is key: you don't determine the MVP on your own. The MVP is the most critical deliverable the business needs—but defining it requires collaboration with your stakeholders. It's not about what you assume is important; it's about uncovering what the business truly needs in that moment.

Collaborating on Priorities

Early in my career, I thought I had the superpower of knowing what mattered most. Turns out, I didn't. I'd look at the list of tasks, assume I knew which one was most critical, and dive right in. But here's the truth: if you don't take the time to talk to your stakeholders, you might be spending hours on something that could wait while ignoring the real business need.

I felt like I was spinning ten plates in the air, confident I had them balanced—until one crashed to the ground. Then another. I was halfway through what I thought was the "critical" part of a project when my phone rang. My boss asked bluntly, "Where are we on the initiative for the client's review tomorrow?" My stomach sank. Turns out, I had misjudged what the stakeholders really needed, and I had spent days working on something that could have been deferred.

That was the moment I realized my priorities weren't always the business's priorities. From then on, I made it my mission to communicate early and often. I began asking stakeholders a critical set of questions: What's the top priority? What's non-negotiable? And—most importantly—what can wait? It wasn't always an easy conversation, but it was crucial to avoid wasting time on the wrong things.

Here's what worked: I'd create a clear timeline outlining what could realistically be delivered by the deadline and then collaborate with stakeholders to finalize the MVP. Once you have clarity on that, everything else becomes easier to manage.

Learning to Say No (Even to Yourself)

Here's the hard part: learning to say no. Not just to others, but to yourself. We all fall into the trap of thinking we can handle it all—and that saying "no" means failure.

I used to be that person who said "yes" to everything, no matter how overwhelmed I already felt. I thought it would show leadership how dedicated I was, how capable I could be. Instead, I became overwhelmed, under-delivered, and started missing deadlines.

This is where MVP thinking comes back into play. Break tasks into smaller pieces wherever possible. Deliver the core essential (MVP), communicate that it's done, and follow up with enhancements later. This approach doesn't just make you more efficient—it shows leadership that you can handle pressure, make smart decisions, and still deliver quality.

Chad, of course, had figured this out long before I did. But let's be real—Chad's "prioritization" strategy was more about making time for mid-week rooftop cocktails than for work. Once I stopped focusing on what he was doing (or not doing), I realized the lesson here was less about being like Chad and more about learning to stop taking on everything.

Communicating Your Priorities

It's one thing to manage your own workload, but what happens when your boss says, "I need this yesterday"? That's where communication becomes key.

I would just nod, smile, and quietly tack the task onto my already-overloaded plate. Staying late felt like the only option. But that's not sustainable, and more often than not, it leads to missed deadlines and unnecessary stress.

What I came to understand is this: leadership isn't just about delivering; it's about setting realistic expectations.

When a new task comes in, be transparent about what you're already working on. Lay out your current workload, offer a realistic timeline, and suggest what can be reprioritized.

In fact, most leaders will appreciate it when you lay out your priorities and suggest a plan that works for everyone. It's about managing expectations, not trying to be a superhero.

This is where Chad's calm demeanor really made sense. He didn't panic when something new landed on his desk because he knew how to negotiate timelines. He wasn't afraid to push back, politely of course, if it meant maintaining the quality of his work.

The lesson here? Don't just say yes; outline how the task affects your current workload. It's not weakness—it's leadership.

The Takeaway

Effective prioritization means acknowledging that you can't do everything—and that's okay. It's about identifying the work that truly moves the needle and communicating those priorities clearly to your stakeholders. Saying "no" to certain tasks or delegating them is not a sign of weakness but a strategic decision to focus on what matters most. Success isn't measured by how much you can juggle but by the impact of the work you choose to deliver.

Action Plan: Prioritizing in a World of Chaos

Objective: Manage your workload effectively by focusing on high-impact tasks, collaborating with stakeholders, and maintaining clarity around shifting priorities.

Framework: Apply this framework to effectively prioritize tasks, focus on high-impact work, and maintain balance in a demanding environment.

1. Identify Urgent, Important, and Dependent Work

Not all tasks deserve equal attention. Tasks impacting other teams or projects ("Dependent" work) should be prioritized to avoid becoming a bottleneck. Beyond "Urgent" or "Important," regularly review and adjust priorities with stakeholders to ensure alignment.

Example: If one task is urgent but another impacts a cross-functional deadline, prioritize the dependent task first to keep the project moving smoothly.

2. Define Your Minimum Viable Product (MVP)

Focus on the deliverable that meets essential needs without overextending. Clarify the MVP with stakeholders to ensure alignment, especially during tight deadlines or limited resources. Delivering the MVP reassures stakeholders while deferring less-critical elements.

Example: On a tight deadline, identify three key components of your current project that deliver the most value. Communicate this plan to stakeholders to align expectations.

3. Delegate Tasks When Possible

Maximize your value by focusing on tasks only you can do while delegating others to your team. Delegation empowers your colleagues and ensures overall efficiency. Highlight the task's importance when delegating to keep them engaged.

Example: Pass a research task to a team member eager to learn, allowing you to focus on finalizing a critical report.

4. Communicate When Priorities Shift

Transparency is essential when unexpected tasks disrupt your workflow. Update stakeholders on current priorities and discuss feasible timelines. Clear communication avoids over-committing and demonstrates leadership.

Example: If your manager adds a high-priority task, outline your current workload and suggest which tasks can be postponed or reassigned to accommodate the new request.

5. Recharge to Stay Effective

Taking short breaks prevents burnout and keeps your mind sharp for high-priority tasks. Protect these moments to recharge and maintain focus during a busy day.

Example: Schedule 10-minute breaks after two hours of focused work. Use the time for a quick walk, coffee, or mindfulness exercise to return with renewed energy.

Reflection and Self-Monitoring

Weekly Reflection: "What was my most significant priority this week, and how well did I manage dependencies?"

Monthly Reflection: Reflect on how effectively you communicated priorities. Identify one strategy to improve task delegation or stakeholder alignment next month.

Chapter 3

Communication and Transparency – Speak Now or Forever Hold Your Stress

Do you often think that as long as you're doing your job well, there's no need to speak up? Ever catch yourself thinking, "If there's a problem, will someone tell me?" Well, let me tell you: silence may be golden in a library, but in the corporate world, it's anything but. Communication—especially about risks and updates—isn't just important; it's critical. Mastering it can be the difference between seizing success and missing out entirely.

The Illusion of Communication

One of my mentors used to tell me, "Most problems in the workplace happen because people think they've communicated when they really haven't." And he was right. In my early days, I thought that sending an email or having a quick chat meant I'd done my part. I assumed that everyone understood what I was saying and would act accordingly. **Big Mistake.**

That's when I learned the value of what I call "overcommunication." No, it's not about flooding inboxes with emails. It's about making sure your message truly lands—by reiterating key points, confirming understanding, and following up as needed. Trust me, overcommunication beats assuming you've said enough, especially when things can go sideways.

Using the right tools can make all the difference in today's remote work landscape. Platforms like Slack, Teams, or Zoom allow you to keep quick updates flowing, create channels for specific projects, and ensure that no one misses a beat—even when working across time zones. However, the tools are only as effective as the intention behind them. Sometimes, a well-timed video call can clear up misunderstandings that a dozen Slack messages might only muddy.

The Importance of Transparency

I once worked under a leader who was a master of transparency. They didn't shy away from sharing bad news or admitting when they didn't have all the answers. They made sure everyone was on the same page, even when the page didn't have the best news written on it. What I learned from that leader is that transparency builds trust, even when you're delivering less-than-ideal updates.

Contrast that with my younger self: I'd wait until issues were at a boiling point before looping in my team or boss. I thought I could fix everything before anyone noticed. That did not end well. The longer I held back bad news, the worse things became. I learned the hard way that the only surprises people like are the ones that come with cake.

Being transparent doesn't just mean sharing problems—it means raising potential issues before they snowball. It means letting your stakeholders know, "Hey, if we don't get this information by next Tuesday, our timeline is at risk." People appreciate the heads-up, even if it's not what they want to hear, because it gives them time to adjust.

Building a Communication Plan

Before any project kicks off, having a communication plan can save a lot of headaches down the road. I learned this the hard way after a project went south because key stakeholders weren't kept in the loop. Creating a simple plan can make a world of difference. Here's what it should include:

- **Identifying Key Stakeholders**: Who needs to be informed? Think beyond your immediate team—consider executives, project sponsors, and cross-functional partners.
- **Setting Communication Frequency**: How often do updates need to be shared? Daily for some, weekly for

others, and maybe just a high-level summary once a month for top leadership.

- **Tailoring Your Message**: Different audiences require different levels of detail. Executives want to know the impact on timelines and budgets, while the project team needs to hear about the nitty-gritty.

By setting these up front, you avoid the trap of leaving people in the dark—or worse, overloading them with information they don't need.

Framing Risks Correctly

Here's a common mistake I made early on: downplaying risks. I'd say things like, "If this vendor doesn't respond soon, it might delay us." Notice the word **"might"**? It made the issue sound optional, and it led to confusion when things inevitably went wrong. What I should have said was, "If we don't get a response from this vendor by Thursday, our deliverable is at risk." It's direct, specific, and doesn't leave room for misinterpretation.

The next time you encounter a potential issue, try framing it with a clear action and consequence. For example, "If we don't receive the feedback from Team X by the end of the week, we'll need to extend the timeline." This approach doesn't just highlight the problem; it frames the urgency and gives your stakeholders a chance to address it before it's too late.

Managing Frustration and Conflict

Change, especially when unexpected, can lead to frustration and even conflicts within the team. I recall a project where, halfway through, the scope changed dramatically. Suddenly, we had new priorities and a tighter timeline. The team was frustrated; their hard work on previous deliverables seemed tossed aside.

To navigate this, I focused on a few key steps: First, I openly acknowledged the frustration. I said, "I know this shift is tough, and I appreciate all the effort you've put in so far." Sometimes, just validating how people feel can go a long way. Then, I clearly communicated why the change was happening and what the new expectations were. And most importantly, I listened to their concerns and made adjustments where possible, showing them that their feedback mattered.

Managing change isn't just about directing traffic—it's about understanding that behind every task is a person who's put in effort, and they deserve to know why their work is shifting direction.

Why Overcommunication Is the Key

Over time, I've come to realize that overcommunication is a form of insurance. It ensures that when things go sideways, you've got a record showing that risks were flagged, decisions were communicated, and everyone had the opportunity to speak up. It's not about creating a paper trail for the sake of it; it's about making sure that when something slips, no one's caught off guard.

And speaking of things slipping, let's talk about Chad. Chad, bless his heart, believed that saying things once—no matter how vaguely—was enough. He figured that if he mentioned a potential delay in passing during a meeting, his job was done. But when that delay turned into a missed deadline, he found himself facing a lot of "Why didn't you say anything?" questions.

Meanwhile, I had started sharing updates regularly—even when everything was going smoothly. Turns out, people appreciate knowing what's on track just as much as they need to know about potential risks. Keeping those communication lines open made all the difference.

Why Meeting Minutes Matter

When you leave a meeting, it's easy to assume everyone walked away with the same understanding. But misunderstandings happen more often than not. That's why sending out meeting minutes after important discussions is crucial. Meeting minutes aren't just a recap; they're a tool for building accountability. By documenting key decisions, action items, deadlines, and who's responsible for each task, you leave no room for ambiguity. Meeting minutes also serve as a reliable reference point, ensuring everyone stays aligned and focused on the agreed goals long after the meeting ends.

After every important meeting, take a few minutes to send a follow-up email with a clear breakdown of:

- **Key Decisions**: What was agreed upon during the meeting.
- **Action Items**: Specific tasks that need to be completed.
- **Deadlines**: When each action item is due.
- **Owners**: Who is responsible for each task.

By doing this, you create a shared understanding and a paper trail that ensures everyone is aligned.

But what about the stuff that doesn't get discussed in formal meetings? Well, this is where transparency comes into play. It's not just about ensuring your communication is received, but making sure it's heard. Think about those quick chats in the hallway or the impromptu decisions made over a casual call—the "just so you know" moments. They're convenient, but without proper follow-up, they might as well not have happened.

The Importance of Documentation via Email

While quick alignments over calls or chats can be helpful in the moment, they're often insufficient for holding people accountable. The real problem with chats and phone calls is that they aren't easily referable when things go wrong. You might agree on something during a call, but unless it's documented, there's no formal record of what was discussed.

That's why I always recommend following up important conversations with an email. It doesn't have to be long; it just needs to summarize the key points. Think of it as a quick confirmation to make sure everyone's on the same page. This way, if there's ever any confusion or disagreement down the road, you've got a record of what was agreed upon. And trust me, having that email chain can save you a lot of headaches later.

The Takeaway

Clear, honest communication is the backbone of every successful project and team. It's not just about giving updates but about fostering understanding, accountability, and trust. Overcommunicate, tailor your message to your audience, and always surface risks early. In the end, transparency is what keeps teams aligned and projects moving forward, especially when things don't go as planned.

Action Plan: Communicating with Clarity and Confidence

Objective: Foster understanding, accountability, and trust through proactive and transparent communication.

Framework: Follow these steps to improve communication, build trust, and maintain transparency, alignment and accountability

1. Practice Proactive Communication

Address potential challenges early to keep projects on track and demonstrate foresight.

Example: If you anticipate delays due to a dependency, notify your team or manager before it becomes an issue. Proactive updates prevent misunderstandings and create space to adjust plans.

2. Set Clear Expectations

Align with stakeholders by defining specific deliverables, timelines, and mutual expectations for any task or project.

Example: Before starting a new project, confirm with stakeholders what "success" looks like and the timeline for each phase. This ensures everyone shares the same vision.

3. Document Key Decisions and Agreements

Maintain accountability by summarizing decisions, alignments, action items, and ownership after meetings or discussions.

Example: Send a follow-up email after meetings detailing key decisions, action items, deadlines, and responsible parties. This avoids ambiguity and serves as a reference point.

4. Ask Clarifying Questions

Seek precision and understanding when instructions or expectations are unclear. This avoids missteps and unnecessary stress.

Example: If a task seems vague, ask, "Could you clarify the desired outcome or the priority for this task?"

5. Speak Up When Priorities Conflict

Communicate workload challenges to stakeholders when conflicting priorities arise. Suggest adjustments or delegation to ensure balance.

Example: If a new urgent task arises, outline your current workload to your manager and ask, "Which task should take priority, and can we adjust timelines for others?"

6. Build a Human Connection with Colleagues

Strengthen relationships by fostering genuine connections, making collaboration smoother and conflict resolution more direct.

Example: Take a moment to ask colleagues about their day or share a personal update. These small interactions build rapport and trust over time.

Reflection and Self-Monitoring

Weekly Reflection: "What potential challenges can I address proactively this week to avoid future issues?"

Monthly Reflection: "How effectively did I document decisions and clarify expectations? How can I improve transparency and communication with stakeholders next month?"

Chapter 4

Navigating Corporate Politics without Losing Yourself

We've all heard it before: "I don't play office politics." Maybe you've even muttered it under your breath after a frustrating day. But here's the uncomfortable truth: politics in the workplace isn't a game you can choose to sit out. You can't just be a spectator, hoping that hard work alone will carry you to the top. If you've ever thought, "I can't grow because I don't engage in office politics," it's time for a perspective shift.

Office politics doesn't have to mean backstabbing or stepping on others to climb the ladder. It's about understanding the complex web of human dynamics and learning to navigate them with grace and skill. I promise you it's not as painful as it sounds. It is a shift in the mindset of how you use your strengths in the most efficient way to position yourself for success. Let's talk about it.

Political Maneuvering Without Losing Yourself

Steering through office politics doesn't mean you have to lose your integrity or become someone you're not. It's about being savvy in your interactions—knowing who holds the cards and understanding what motivates them. Let's face it: organizations are a mosaic of individuals, each with their own goals, fears, and aspirations. Pretending these dynamics don't exist doesn't make them disappear; it just leaves you unprepared.

Early on, I was convinced that if I just kept my head down and focused on delivering great work, I'd naturally rise through the ranks. Meritocracy at its finest, right? But reality hit hard when promotions passed me by. I learned that success isn't just about your skill set or work ethic; it's also about visibility and having advocates in your corner when key decisions are made.

Take Chad, for example. Chad could work a room like a seasoned politician. He always seemed to be in the right meetings, casually chatting with the higher-ups, positioning himself where the action was. But here's the kicker—even Chad, with all his savvy, wasn't invincible. He built genuine relationships and aligned himself with influential people, but he wasn't immune to missteps.

Building Bridges, Not Walls

The thing about office politics is that it's not a zero-sum game. Your success doesn't require someone else's failure. In fact, the most effective leaders I've met are those who make allies, not enemies. Navigating the political landscape is less about outmaneuvering others and more about uniting people toward a shared objective.

I recall a high-stakes project involving multiple departments, each with its own agenda and a few oversized egos in the mix. Tensions were high, and it was clear that without intervention, the project was doomed. My initial instinct was to bury myself in my work and sidestep the drama, but that only made things worse. So, I took a step back and identified the key players. I listened to their concerns, understood what each person needed to feel valued, and started building bridges. By facilitating small compromises, we got everyone back on track without anyone feeling like they'd lost ground.

You don't have to become a schemer to navigate office politics effectively. It's about fostering connections and finding common ground to align everyone's interests.

Practical Diplomacy 101

So, how do you actually do this? Think of political navigation as practicing diplomacy rather than manipulation. The goal is to engage others while staying true to yourself. Here are some practical tips:

- **Listen more than you talk**: Understanding the lay of the land is critical before you dive in. Pay attention to what motivates people around you. What are they trying to achieve? Where do their interests align with yours? Listening allows you to respond strategically.

- **Frame your requests carefully**: Don't just walk into meetings demanding things. Frame your ideas in a way that appeals to what others value. For instance, if you need help from a colleague, position your request in terms of how it helps the team or organization as a whole, not just you.

- **Don't get drawn into drama**: It's easy to be pulled into office gossip or conflicts. Stay out of the fray. Political maneuvering isn't about taking sides in petty disputes—it's about rising above the noise and staying focused on your goals.

Finding Your Tribe

Every workplace has its cliques and circles of influence. Aligning yourself with the right people can open doors you didn't even know existed. But this isn't about brown-nosing or sacrificing your authenticity; it's about finding your tribe within the organization.

For me, it meant connecting with colleagues who shared similar values—ambitious yet ethical individuals who aimed for company growth without cutting corners. As I built relationships with these like-minded people, opportunities started to surface more organically. Being part of this network provided access to resources, support, and increased visibility.

However, there's a fine line. It's easy to spread yourself too thin by trying to be everything to everyone, which can leave you exhausted and less effective. Balancing relationship-building with delivering tangible results is crucial.

Building a Reputation for Reliability

Another vital lesson I've learned is the importance of building a reputation for reliability and supportiveness. People may forget the specifics of your accomplishments, but they'll always remember how you made them feel and whether you were there when they needed you. This kind of reputation is gold, especially when navigating office politics with integrity. It's one thing to be ambitious; it's another to be the go-to person when challenges arise.

By consistently delivering and supporting your colleagues, you position yourself as a trustworthy and valuable team member. This not only fosters goodwill but also enhances your influence within the organization.

Chad's Political Fumble

Let me share a story about Chad's misstep that offers a valuable lesson. Chad, usually sharp in navigating politics, let overconfidence lead him down the wrong path. We were on a project involving two major stakeholders. Chad bet heavily on one, convinced that this person held all the cards.

He sidelined the other stakeholder, assuming they lacked real influence. But when decisions were made, that overlooked stakeholder turned out to have significant sway. Chad's strategy backfired spectacularly, costing him the leadership role on the project and damaging his credibility.

The takeaway? Effective political navigation requires a comprehensive understanding of the entire landscape. It's not enough to align with the most prominent figure; you need to manage relationships with all influential parties, visible or not. Chad learned the hard way that neglecting key relationships can lead to significant setbacks.

Why Relationships Matter More Than You Think

We all like to think that hard work and talent are the sole drivers of success, but relationships play an equally crucial role. They can open doors that effort alone cannot. Building authentic connections—with superiors, peers, and even subordinates—can yield dividends far into the future.

This brings us back to the importance of nurturing both upward and downward networks. Having supporters at all levels who can vouch for you is invaluable. And let's not forget your peers; when challenges arise, they're the ones who can either rally to your aid or leave you to fend for yourself.

Political Navigation with Integrity

You might think that engaging in office politics requires compromising your values, but that's a misconception. When done correctly, political navigation is about being authentic while strategic. It's about understanding the organizational dynamics and leveraging them ethically to achieve your goals.

I've learned that you don't have to "play dirty" to advance. Building genuine relationships, offering help, and strategically aligning with others can all be done while maintaining your integrity. In fact, this approach is not only ethical but also more sustainable in the long run.

The Takeaway

Office politics are inevitable, but they don't have to be a negative force. The key is to navigate them with integrity, forging relationships that propel everyone forward, not just yourself. By practicing diplomacy, actively listening, and framing your requests to resonate with others, you can advance without sacrificing your values. Remember, true success in the political landscape isn't about outmaneuvering others; it's about aligning goals and finding common ground.

Action Plan: Navigating Corporate Politics with Integrity

Objective: Build influence and navigate workplace dynamics with diplomacy and authenticity, aligning goals and fostering trust.

Framework: Use the steps below to engage with workplace dynamics thoughtfully, build meaningful relationships, and maintain your integrity while navigating office politics.

1. Build Alliances, Not Rivalries

Turn conflicts into opportunities to build trust by collaborating on solutions rather than assigning blame.

Example: During a team project, address a missed deadline collaboratively by reaching out to the responsible party and proposing solutions. This builds goodwill and strengthens alliances.

2. Communicate Diplomatically

Frame your requests around shared goals by understanding others' motivations and priorities.

Example: When seeking support from a resistant colleague, begin by asking about their challenges. Use their input to tailor your proposal, showing how it aligns with their objectives.

3. Build a Network Aligned with Your Values

Focus on relationships with colleagues who share your commitment to growth and integrity, creating a support system that reflects your principles.

Example: Identify three colleagues whose values align with yours and actively engage with them through regular check-ins or shared projects. A like-minded network offers authentic and reliable support.

4. Balance Relationships Across Stakeholders

Avoid relying on a single ally by engaging with all relevant stakeholders and understanding their influence on your projects.

Example: During a cross-functional project, ensure you connect with multiple leaders and team members. This prevents dependence on one person and strengthens your overall support network.

Reflection and Self-Monitoring

Weekly Reflection: "What steps did I take this week to build alliances or strengthen my network?"

Monthly Reflection: "How balanced are my relationships across stakeholders? What actions can I take to build stronger connections where needed?"

Section 2

Self-Mastery and Personal Growth

Chapter 5

Learning from Mistakes – Growth Through Failure

In the early stages of my career, I was convinced that perfection was the pathway to success. Mistakes were obstacles to be avoided at all costs, signs of weakness that could derail my progress. However, I soon realized that this mindset was not only unrealistic but also limiting. Embracing failure isn't a setback; it's a stepping stone toward growth and innovation.

Consider Chad. He had an interesting approach to failure: "If I don't acknowledge it, it doesn't exist." While the rest of us scrambled to address our errors, Chad maintained an air of effortless confidence. It was as if he floated above the turmoil unaffected. But the reality was that unresolved issues have a way of resurfacing, and Chad wasn't immune to their consequences. Let me talk you through my experience.

Own Your Mistakes Before They Own You

Every time we make a mistake, we're presented with a choice: conceal it or confront it. In my early days, I often chose to hide my errors, thinking I could correct them unnoticed and preserve my reputation. I believed that admitting mistakes was a sign of weakness. However, I learned that hiding mistakes not only exacerbates them but also erodes trust among your colleagues and superiors.

One incident stands out vividly. I was leading a critical project with tight deadlines. In my eagerness to deliver, I overlooked some early warning signs—minor issues that I thought I could resolve on my own. Instead of seeking input, I doubled down, working longer hours in isolation. By the time I realized the problem was beyond my capacity, it had escalated into a major setback. Had I addressed it openly from the start, the team could have collaborated on a solution, preventing the crisis altogether.

Chad, on the other hand, perfected the art of denial. When things went awry, he'd carry on as if everything was fine, deflecting any signs of trouble. His composure was almost enviable. But unresolved mistakes have a way of catching up, and Chad's avoidance strategy eventually led to bigger problems that affected not just him but the entire team.

For Everyone, Leadership or Not: Ask for Help

You don't need to be in a leadership position to face this dilemma. Whether you're a project manager, an analyst, or new to the workforce, the principle remains: hiding mistakes doesn't work. Pretending everything is fine when it's not only exacerbates the problem. The key to navigating errors—regardless of your role—is understanding that asking for help isn't a weakness; it's a strength.

If you're not yet in a leadership role, remember this: your network is your greatest asset. Cultivate relationships where you can seek advice and assistance before things go awry. Don't wait for someone else to step in. Leverage your peers, mentors, and anyone who can offer perspective before a minor issue escalates.

I once tried to tackle a complex data integration task solo, believing that sheer effort would get me through. After hours of frustration, I finally reached out to a colleague who'd dealt with similar challenges. He provided a simple solution that saved me hours of work—and prevented a potential mistake. The lesson? Don't wait until the last minute to ask for help. Whether you're leading or following, early communication makes finding solutions much easier.

Chad, however, never asked for help. Why would he when everything seemed fine? *(even though it wasn't.)* It's easy to think that seeking assistance makes you appear less competent. In reality, it shows you're committed to getting things right.

Failure: The Best (and Worst) Teacher

Accepting that failure is not a dead-end but a detour on the path to success is challenging. Yet, failure can be the most effective teacher if you're open to its lessons. Reflecting on my project disaster, I initially felt embarrassed and defeated. But in hindsight, it was a pivotal moment that reshaped my approach to work and leadership.

By acknowledging my mistakes openly, I was able to analyze the root causes. The project didn't fail due to a single error but a series of small misjudgments—delayed communication, reluctance to seek advice, and failure to leverage my network. Recognizing these patterns was crucial for my personal and professional growth.

In the midst of challenges, it's tempting to adopt a lone-wolf mentality, especially when we believe that leaders should have all the answers. However, true leadership involves recognizing when to draw on the strengths of others. One of the most valuable lessons I've learned is that seeking help is a sign of wisdom, not weakness. Utilizing your network can transform obstacles into opportunities.

Chad, despite his avoidance tactics, did have one admirable quality: he didn't let failure immobilize him. He moved forward regardless of setbacks. However, his flaw was in pretending the failures didn't exist at all. The key difference lies in acknowledging mistakes and using them as a foundation for improvement.

Shyam Uthaman

The Power of Admitting Mistakes Early

One crucial lesson often overlooked in management is the importance of early admission of mistakes. Addressing issues promptly can safeguard your project and preserve trust. I recall delaying the disclosure of a significant risk, believing I could resolve it independently. By the time I involved others, the issue had escalated unnecessarily, complicating the resolution process.

This is where overcommunication becomes invaluable. While it may feel uncomfortable to highlight potential problems, proactive transparency prevents minor issues from becoming major crises. Teams and stakeholders prefer early warnings over unexpected emergencies, allowing for collaborative problem-solving and contingency planning.

Had I practiced overcommunication, I could have leveraged my team's collective expertise to address the problem earlier. My hesitation not only intensified the issue but also strained relationships and trust within the team.

Chad, on the other hand, avoided the discomfort altogether by not addressing issues at all. He moved on quickly, leaving others to deal with the fallout. The lesson is clear: it's far better to confront mistakes early than to deal with compounded problems later.

Failing Forward: Turning Setbacks into Learning Moments

In the aftermath of the failed project, I faced a crossroads: succumb to discouragement or transform the experience into a learning opportunity. Choosing the latter, I convened my team for an open discussion. "What can we learn from this?" I asked. This shift in perspective marked the beginning of a new approach to challenges.

Together, we conducted a thorough analysis of what went wrong. We identified breakdowns in communication, gaps in our processes, and missed opportunities for collaboration. It became evident that many missteps were preventable. This collaborative reflection not only provided valuable insights but also strengthened our team's cohesion.

The experience underscored the importance of valuing input from all team members. Those on the front lines often have a clearer view of emerging issues. By fostering an environment where everyone feels comfortable sharing concerns and suggestions, you transform setbacks into collective growth opportunities.

Chad avoided retrospection altogether. For him, completed projects were left in the past, devoid of analysis. This approach meant missing out on valuable lessons that could inform future success. In contrast, embracing reflection enabled me to turn failures into catalysts for improvement.

Ending on the Lesson: Learn, Grow, and Move Forward

Mistakes are an unavoidable part of any professional journey. The critical factor is not the mistakes themselves but our response to them. By owning up to errors, seeking assistance, and viewing failures as learning opportunities, we cultivate resilience and continuous improvement.

Chad's avoidance strategy may offer temporary relief, but it hinders long-term growth. Embracing mistakes, extracting lessons, and applying them moving forward is the sustainable path to success. Failure becomes a stepping stone rather than a stumbling block when we allow it to educate us.

The Takeaway

Failure is not the antithesis of success but an integral component of it. It's through confronting and learning from our mistakes that we refine our strategies, strengthen our character, and achieve lasting success. Own your mistakes, embrace the lessons they offer, and encourage your team to do the same. Remember, failure only becomes a permanent setback if you allow it to be.

Action Plan: Turning Mistakes into Growth Opportunities

Objective: Leverage mistakes for growth by taking responsibility, seeking support early, fostering a culture of learning, and building trust through transparency.

Framework: Apply these steps to turn mistakes into valuable learning opportunities, building resilience and driving personal and professional growth.

1. Take Responsibility and Communicate Early

Address challenges proactively to prevent minor issues from escalating into larger problems.

Example: On a project where I missed initial warning signs, I delayed raising the issue until it impacted our timeline. If I had communicated the risk earlier, the team could have collaborated on a solution before it escalated.

2. Seek Support Before Challenges Become Crises

Reach out for help early when facing challenges that aren't easily resolved, leveraging the expertise of your network.

Example: When I struggled with a complex task, I hesitated to ask for advice and wasted hours. Once I sought help, a colleague provided a simple solution that saved time and reduced risk.

3. Create a Learning Culture After Setbacks

Foster team discussions after setbacks to turn mistakes into shared learning opportunities that strengthen processes and accountability

Example: After a failed project, I led a review session where we analyzed mistakes objectively. This discussion improved team morale and helped us refine our approach for future projects.

4. Be Transparent While Safeguarding Credibility

Share challenges openly, framing them as lessons or collaborative opportunities to maintain trust and minimize lame.

Example: When sharing a setback, I focused on team goals and process improvements, explaining the lesson learned and the corrective actions. This built trust while emphasizing my proactive approach.

Reflection and Self-Monitoring

Weekly Reflection: "What mistakes or potential challenges did I identify this week, and how did I address them?"

Monthly Reflection: "How effectively did I communicate and learn from setbacks? What steps can I take to improve transparency and collaboration in the future?"

Chapter 6

Reinventing Yourself – Sailing Where the Wind Blows

There was a time when I thought I was at the top of my game—or at least, that's what I believed. I had honed a particular skill over the years; it was my specialty, the kind that gets you noticed. For a while, it did. I received praise, exciting projects, and plenty of pats on the back. But one day, I looked around and realized the landscape had changed. The projects that once came my way were drying up, and the skills I was so proud of were no longer in high demand.

Initially, I blamed everything but myself. "Why is Chad getting all the good opportunities? Why are they promoting people in that department? They barely even know what they're doing!" But then it hit me—while I was busy perfecting my niche, Chad and others were diversifying. They were picking up new skills, moving into new areas, and positioning themselves where the company was growing.

That's when I learned one of the hardest lessons in corporate life: being great at something today doesn't guarantee you'll be relevant tomorrow. Sometimes, the wind changes direction, and you either adapt or get left behind.

The Problem with Staying in One Lane

We like to believe that if we keep improving our craft, the world will reward us. It's comforting to think that being an expert in one area secures our place in the company. But that's not always how it works. Markets shift, industries evolve, and what was once essential can become obsolete.

At one point, I was known as the "go-to" person for a specific technical skill. It was niche, and I took pride in being the best at it. But gradually, I noticed that while I was sharpening my expertise, the company was investing in new technologies and branching into different markets. The projects that once depended on my skills were fading, and I found myself watching from the sidelines.

Cue Chad. He wasn't just "that guy" everyone knew; he was the one who saw where the company was heading before the rest of us caught on. While I was refining what I knew, Chad was out there learning new skills. And, naturally, he made sure everyone knew it.

"Hey, did you hear we're rolling out that new initiative? I'm already working with the team on it." Classic Chad.

Sailing Where the Wind Blows

A mentor once told me, "Sail where the wind is blowing, not against it." Simple words, but profound wisdom. In the corporate world, this means looking ahead and aligning your skills with where the company is growing. Those who thrive aren't necessarily the best at their current roles; they're the ones gearing up for the next big opportunity.

This doesn't mean you have to abandon your strengths, but it does require a willingness to reinvent yourself. I began exploring in-demand skills and the company's future direction. Was I comfortable with it? Not entirely. Did it feel like starting over? In some ways, yes. But I realized that clinging to my comfort zone wouldn't take me where I wanted to go.

So, I took the plunge—signed up for new projects, acquired new skills, and—even though it pained me—started following Chad's lead. He wasn't just skating by; he was staying relevant. And I needed to do the same.

Pivoting Isn't Failure

Many of us harbor an unspoken fear about changing course. It can feel like admitting defeat, like acknowledging, "Maybe I wasn't as good as I thought." But it's not about abandoning your strengths; it's about expanding your toolkit.

I've witnessed talented individuals cling tightly to their familiar skills, only to miss out on new opportunities because they feared starting over. The hard truth is, if you wait too long, the world doesn't wait with you—it moves on. Reinventing yourself is about staying in the game, not watching from the bleachers.

If I've learned anything from Chad, it's that flexibility is a form of power. And no, Chad hasn't become my hero—he's still that guy. But I've realized there's value in borrowing a page from his playbook. Reinventing yourself doesn't erase past successes; it ensures you're equipped for future relevance.

The Takeaway

So, what's the lesson? Reinvention isn't a luxury; it's a necessity. You can't depend on yesterday's successes to keep you relevant tomorrow. Look forward, embrace learning, and sail where the wind takes you. And if you ever catch yourself wondering how Chad stays ahead, remember—sometimes, Chad has a point. Adapt, or get left behind.

Action Plan: Reinventing Yourself to Stay Relevant

Objective: Follow the below framework to adapt to changing landscapes, expand your skill set, and position yourself for future opportunities by staying proactive and flexible.

Framework: These steps will help you identify when to pivot, embrace change, and align your evolving skills with future opportunities while maintaining your core strengths.

1. Recognize When It's Time to Pivot

Regularly evaluate the relevance of your current skills and identify areas where the company or industry is heading.

Example: I noticed a decline in projects aligned with my expertise, prompting me to explore emerging skills and take on projects in growing areas.

2. Embrace Change as a Strength

View learning new skills as a growth opportunity rather than a loss of your comfort zone.

Example: Initially, transitioning to a new area felt like starting over. However, reframing it as an expansion of my expertise helped me tackle the challenge positively.

3. Proactively Seek Growth Opportunities

Volunteer for projects that align with future trends and company goals to position yourself for upcoming opportunities.

Example: Observing colleagues involved in innovative initiatives inspired me to join similar projects, which increased my visibility and kept me relevant.

4. Lean on Mentors and Peers for Guidance

Seek advice from those who have successfully navigated similar transitions to gain insights and avoid common pitfalls.

Example: I consulted mentors adapting to emerging trends, who provided guidance on valuable skills and practical learning approaches.

5. Integrate Core Skills with New Knowledge

Combine your existing expertise with new skills to enhance versatility without abandoning your strengths.

Example: I found ways to blend my technical knowledge with new tools and approaches, creating unique contributions that showcased both my legacy and growth.

Reflection and Self-Monitoring

Weekly Reflection: "What skills or trends have I noticed growing in importance, and how can I start exploring them?"

Monthly Reflection: "How effectively am I integrating new knowledge with my existing expertise? What additional steps can I take to align with future opportunities?"

Chapter 7

Overcoming Impostor Syndrome and Self-Doubt

I remember the day I was promoted to a major leadership role—the kind I'd been striving for, the one that would finally seat me among the key decision-makers. Colleagues congratulated me, assuring me I deserved it, and for a fleeting moment, I believed them. But as weeks passed, an unsettling doubt began to creep in. I started questioning whether I was truly ready for the role. It wasn't an immediate feeling, but over time, it gnawed at me like a persistent itch I couldn't quite reach.

Being younger than most of the team I managed—many with decades of experience—I couldn't help but wonder, "How did I get here so quickly?" The nagging thought that I'd somehow slipped through the cracks and fooled everyone into believing I belonged haunted me. "What if they find out I'm not as capable as they think?" I'd ask myself. And just like that, impostor syndrome took hold.

The Persistent Doubt

The peculiar thing about impostor syndrome is that it doesn't correlate with actual competence. You could be excelling beyond everyone else and still feel like a fraud. The worst part? That doubt begins to influence your actions. You shrink yourself, second-guess decisions, and hold back from speaking up because a voice inside whispers, "Who am I to offer advice when others know so much more?"

Chad, naturally, never appeared to grapple with such doubts. He could stride into any room, make the most off-the-wall statement, and still carry himself as if delivering a keynote speech. Confidence was never his shortcoming. Despite spending much of my career rolling my eyes at him, I've often wondered—what would it be like to possess even a sliver of that self-assuredness?

The Internal Battle

Impostor syndrome feels like an invisible anchor, dragging you down and hindering your best work because you're terrified others will "discover" you're not as competent as they believe. But here's the reality: no one will "find you out" unless you undermine yourself. Often, it's our own self-doubt that holds us back, not external judgments.

After that promotion, impostor syndrome hit me hard. Every decision felt scrutinized. I'd lie awake replaying meetings, dissecting every comment I made, worrying if I appeared competent. The anxiety was palpable. There was a moment when I even contemplated stepping down, convinced I was in over my head.

Reality Check

But then, a realization dawned on me. During a meeting where a project I knew inside and out was being discussed, I recognized that I genuinely knew my stuff. I'd invested the time, done the hard work, and my input was valued because I'd earned my place. I wasn't a fluke or an imposter; I was there for a reason.

That's the insidious nature of impostor syndrome—it's seldom grounded in reality. It's an internal narrative convincing us we're inadequate. But when you step back and assess the facts, you realize that doubting voice isn't as trustworthy as it seems.

Changing the Narrative

So, how do you combat it? For me, it began with changing the narrative. Instead of fixating on what I might lack, I started focusing on what I brought to the table. I made it a habit to acknowledge my successes, no matter how small. Each time I resolved an issue or led a productive meeting, I'd remind myself, "You've got this."

Another strategy that helped was opening up to those who'd been in my shoes. I confided in a mentor about feeling out of place, and to my surprise, he chuckled—not at me, but at the notion that I was alone in this feeling. "Everyone experiences that," he assured me. "You think Chad doesn't feel that sometimes? The key is not letting it hold you back."

That was eye-opening. Chad—the same guy who suggested we "circle back" on the main agenda item during a meeting—even he felt like an impostor at times? If Chad could experience self-doubt yet still forge ahead, perhaps there was a lesson there for me.

Pushing Through Doubt

What I learned is that overcoming impostor syndrome doesn't eradicate doubt entirely. Doubts will resurface, but it's about pushing through them. You don't have to feel fully confident to be effective. Sometimes, you have to act the part until genuine confidence follows.

Now, when doubts creep in, I pause and ask myself, "What would I tell someone else in my shoes?" Almost always, the advice is clear: you've earned your place. You're here for a reason. Don't let that inner critic prevent you from owning your accomplishments.

The Takeaway

Impostor syndrome is a common, albeit deceptive, feeling that can hinder your progress if allowed. Success isn't about the absence of doubt; it's about advancing in spite of it. Acknowledge your worth, focus on the value you contribute, and remember that overcoming self-doubt hinges on action—accumulating small victories that bolster confidence over time. Surround yourself with supportive individuals, lean on them when doubt arises, but never let it stall your journey.

Action Plan: Building Confidence and Conquering Self-Doubt

Objective: Use the steps below to manage self-doubt, build confidence, and shift your mindset toward recognizing your value and embracing your accomplishments.

Framework: These steps will help you reframe your mindset, leverage support systems, and take deliberate actions to overcome self-doubt and build enduring confidence.

1. Reframe Your Achievements

Focus on what you've accomplished instead of dwelling on perceived shortcomings. Acknowledge wins—big or small—as evidence of your capabilities.

Example: After my promotion, I questioned whether I was ready for the role. By reflecting on past successes, I shifted my mindset and recognized that my contributions were earned, not luck.

2. Lean on Mentors for Perspective

Open up to trusted mentors or colleagues about your doubts. Their experiences can help normalize your feelings and provide valuable insights.

Example: A mentor once told me that even seasoned leaders face impostor syndrome. This conversation helped me realize that self-doubt is common and conquerable.

3. Project Confidence (With Preparation)

Project confidence even if you don't fully feel it yet. Preparation and a focus on facts can help you act assuredly until true confidence follows. "Fake it till you make it" does work and works well indeed.

Example: Early on, I hesitated to speak up in meetings. By preparing thoroughly and adopting a confident tone, I gained credibility and eventually grew into the role.

4. Shift the Narrative of Self-Doubt

Challenge negative self-talk by reframing your inner dialogue to focus on strengths and successes rather than perceived weaknesses.

Example: When I doubted myself, I listed recent accomplishments and skills, which helped me recognize my true capabilities and silence unhelpful self-criticism.

5. Push Forward with Small Wins

Set achievable goals that stretch your comfort zone. Each small success reinforces your confidence and builds momentum for larger achievements.

Example: Taking on incremental challenges—like leading a meeting or proposing a solution—helped me prove my abilities to myself, one step at a time.

Reflection and Self-Monitoring

Weekly Reflection: "What actions did I take this week to challenge self-doubt, and how did they reinforce my confidence?"

Monthly Reflection: "What achievements and small wins can I celebrate this month? How can I continue pushing forward despite doubts?"

Chapter 8

Building Resilience and Maintaining Sanity

I'd love to claim that I've always managed stress effortlessly, but there have been moments when I've stared blankly at my computer screen, gripped by silent panic. Deadlines looming, projects slipping, and an incessant flood of emails clamoring for attention. Meanwhile, Chad appeared unflappable, navigating everything with ease. But the truth is, Chad experienced stress too; he just approached it differently.

Building resilience in the corporate jungle is akin to building muscle—each time you push through strain, you grow stronger. But the real skill lies in knowing when to push and when to step back before things unravel.

Resilience didn't come naturally to me. Early on, I thought the remedy for stress was to double down—longer hours, skipping breaks, fueling up on caffeine. It seemed effective for a time. Until it wasn't. The issue with that method is that you eventually slam into a wall. Burnout isn't merely about fatigue; it's a profound exhaustion where even contemplating work becomes overwhelming.

The Burnout Trap

I remember one particular week when everything seemed to be going off the rails. The project I was overseeing lagged behind schedule, the client grew restless, and I was clocking 14-hour days just to keep things from sinking. It felt like no matter how hard I pushed, I was perpetually one step behind.

Meanwhile, Chad—of course—wasn't floundering in stress. He seemed to have discovered a sweet spot between productivity and self-care. He left the office on time, remained composed during intense meetings, and even scheduled his breaks like a corporate zen master. That's when it hit me—Chad wasn't superhuman; he simply knew when to step back.

Resilience isn't about relentless pushing; it's about pacing yourself and understanding how to recharge when pressure mounts.

Setting Boundaries Without Guilt

The initial step in cultivating resilience is mastering the art of setting boundaries. For the longest time, I believed that declining extra work or setting time limits would paint me as uncommitted. I was mistaken. Always saying "yes" led to overcommitment, burnout, and paradoxically, diminished performance.

The lesson here is that setting boundaries isn't shirking responsibility; it's managing it wisely. Attempting to do everything all the time leads to exhaustion and subpar work. Chad seemed to grasp this naturally. He knew when to say, "Let's tackle that tomorrow," while I was burning the midnight oil to stay afloat.

It's not about doing less; it's about prioritizing what matters and safeguarding your mental and physical well-being.

The Importance of Recharging

One of the toughest lessons was recognizing the importance of taking breaks. It seems obvious, but amid a stressful project, self-care often slips. I once viewed powering through as a badge of honor—skipping meals, working weekends, subsisting on coffee.

But the truth is, driving yourself into the ground doesn't yield better outcomes—it leads to burnout. You need time to recharge, to step back from the frenzy, and to clear your mind. It's in those restful moments that clarity emerges, allowing you to return revitalized.

I'll admit, seeing Chad casually leave the office on time while I toiled away made me rethink my strategy. Over time, I realized that taking breaks isn't laziness; it's about sustainability. Chad wasn't untouched by stress; he simply managed it more effectively by knowing when to recharge.

The Real Meaning of "Fake It Till You Make It"

We've all heard the phrase, "Fake it till you make it." But let's clarify—it doesn't mean deceit or feigning expertise. It means embodying the qualities of the person you aim to become, even when it feels uncomfortable or unfamiliar.

When I first assumed a leadership position, I often didn't feel like a leader. I doubted my abilities, second-guessed decisions, and questioned if I was out of my depth. The key wasn't pretending to have all the answers; it was about consistently showing up, putting in the effort, and gradually growing into the role I was qualified for, even if it didn't always feel that way.

It's akin to building resilience. You're not ignoring the existence of stress; you're learning to handle it more effectively each day. Over time, actions like setting boundaries, seeking assistance, and recharging become instinctive, and before you know it, you've "made it." But it's the effort you invest during those challenging times that propels you forward.

Building a Support System

Resilience isn't achieved in isolation. It's also about cultivating a support system. Whether it's your team, friends, or mentors, having a network to lean on during tough times is crucial. I used to think asking for help would make me appear less competent, but in reality, it enhanced my effectiveness.

In my early career, I was awful at delegating. I thought handling everything myself demonstrated competence. But I eventually realized that true success lies in knowing when to ask for help. You don't need to shoulder every burden to validate your value.

Chad, with his relaxed attitude, excelled in this area. He knew when to involve the right people, delegate tasks, and lean on his network when overwhelmed. It wasn't about shirking responsibility; it was about working smarter.

The Takeaway

Building resilience isn't about being impervious to stress; it's about managing it to stay healthy, focused, and effective. Set boundaries, prioritize self-care, and don't hesitate to seek help when needed. And if you ever think Chad has all the answers, remember he's not superhuman—he's just learned to navigate the game differently. Perhaps there's a lesson in that for all of us.

Action Plan: Building Resilience and Managing Stress

Objective: Implement strategies to manage workplace stress, build resilience, and create a sustainable balance for long-term success.

Framework: Apply the following framework to manage workplace stress effectively, build resilience, and create a sustainable balance for long-term success.

1. Set Boundaries to Protect Your Energy

Prioritize high-impact tasks and politely decline work that overextends you, focusing on what delivers the most value. Boundaries preserve energy and enhance performance.

Example: I learned to say no to low-priority tasks by framing them as misaligned with immediate goals, redirecting my time toward impactful work.

2. Recharge Purposefully to Sustain Productivity

Incorporate small, purposeful breaks into your day to sustain focus and clarity. Consistent recharging helps maintain productivity over the long term.

Example: A five-minute walk or brief meditation between meetings helped me clear my mind and return to tasks with renewed energy.

3. Accept Imperfection to Foster Growth

Shift your focus from flawless outcomes to steady progress. Embracing imperfection reduces stress and fosters sustainable growth.

Example: By setting realistic goals and valuing incremental improvements, I reduced the pressure of striving for perfection and achieved more consistent results.

4. Build Support Networks to Share Challenges

Lean on colleagues, mentors, and your network to manage challenges and distribute workload effectively. Resilience grows when responsibilities are shared.

Example: Delegating tasks to team members not only lightened my load but also strengthened collaboration and built trust within the team.

Reflection and Self-Monitoring

Weekly Reflection: "Did I maintain boundaries and take time to recharge this week? How did it impact my focus and stress levels?"

Monthly Reflection: "What improvements can I make in managing stress and building resilience? How can I better utilize my support network?"

Chapter 9

Getting Out of Your Own Way

To be frank, one of the biggest obstacles in my career wasn't a difficult boss, a demanding client, or a challenging project—it was me. Specifically, it was the doubts I nurtured, the fears I allowed to grow, and the tendency to overthink until I was immobilized. It's easy to point fingers when things go awry, but sometimes the real barrier is the person reflected in the mirror.

Let's be honest—we've all sabotaged ourselves at some point. Hesitating to voice an idea, second-guessing decisions, procrastinating on opportunities—self-sabotage wears many masks. The irony is that we're often unaware we're even doing it.

For me, overthinking was the trap. I'd analyze every possible scenario, weigh all potential outcomes, and end up paralyzed by options—doing nothing. Worse yet, I'd deliberate so long that opportunities slipped away. Meanwhile, Chad moved through decisions effortlessly, almost instinctively. He wasn't careless, but he didn't get bogged down in the mental quicksand that often trapped me.

The Overthinking Trap

It's tempting to mistake overthinking for thoroughness. Isn't it wise to consider all options before acting? But there's a fine line between diligent planning and analysis paralysis. When you dwell on every "what if" to the point of inaction, you're trapped.

I recall being tasked with leading a new project outside my usual expertise. I spent hours researching, planning, and crafting detailed proposals, yet never truly began. My obsession with perfection delayed the entire project, exacerbating the situation.

Then there's Chad, who likely would have dived right in, figuring things out as he went and adapting on the fly. As much as I disliked admitting it, that's often the better approach. You don't need all the answers upfront; sometimes, you just need to begin.

Perfectionism: The Sneaky Saboteur

If overthinking didn't stall me, perfectionism did. Perfectionism can masquerade as ambition, but often it's fear dressed up—fear of failure, fear of embarrassment, fear of inadequacy. So instead of releasing work that's "good enough," we wait for perfection—which, unfortunately, never arrives.

I once postponed sending a project update to leadership because I sought flawlessness. I scrutinized every detail, rephrased sentences, and revised the slide deck multiple times. By the time I sent it, I'd missed the deadline and the chance for early feedback. In my quest for perfection, I lost sight of the real goal—progress.

Chad, conversely, grasped that "good enough" moves the needle, and refinement can happen along the way. As much as I once dismissed his method, he was onto something. Progress over perfection—you can't win a race if you never leave the starting line.

The Fear of Failure

At the root of overthinking and perfectionism is fear. Fear is a powerful motivator but also paralyzing if you let it control you. Fear of failing publicly, making the wrong decision, or hearing "I told you so" can make you stay in your comfort zone forever.

But if you're always playing it safe, you're not really playing at all. Every decision comes with risks; every action has the potential for failure. If you let fear dictate your choices, you'll end up exactly where you started—standing still.

I had to learn to stop treating failure as the end. It's part of the journey. In fact, some of the most successful people I know—including Chad—aren't afraid to fail. They understand that failure isn't fatal; it's feedback. The quicker you fail, the quicker you learn, adjust, and try again.

Getting Out of Your Own Way

The moment I recognized that I was my own obstacle, things began to change. I ceased waiting for ideal conditions and started acting. Were all my moves flawless? Absolutely not. Did I experience failures? Yes. But each misstep taught me something valuable. More importantly, I discovered I was more capable than I had believed.

It wasn't about surpassing Chad or anyone else; it was about surpassing the fearful version of myself hesitant to take risks. I stopped allowing fear and overthinking to dictate my story. Instead, I embraced uncertainty, knowing that whatever the outcome, I'd learn and grow.

The Takeaway

Overcoming self-imposed barriers isn't about eradicating fear; it's about managing it and moving forward regardless. Stop waiting for the perfect moment, conditions, or solution. Progress—not perfection—is what propels you toward your goals.

Action Plan: Breaking Through Self-Imposed Barriers

Objective: Overcome overthinking, perfectionism, and fear by taking decisive actions, reframing failure, and embracing uncertainty to unlock your potential.

Framework: Follow these steps to overcome overthinking, perfectionism, and fear, allowing you to take decisive actions and move forward with confidence.

1. Stop Overthinking and Start Acting

Overanalyzing often delays progress. Shifting to a mindset of "progress over perfection" leads to more action and momentum.

Example: Instead of perfecting every detail before starting a project, I limited myself to a brief initial plan and took action. Progress revealed the path forward more effectively than prolonged planning.

2. Set a Quick Decision Deadline

Waiting too long for clarity can result in missed opportunities. Setting a short, self-imposed deadline for decisions builds decisiveness and reduces hesitation.

Example: When faced with a choice, I gave myself five minutes to decide, training my mind to act confidently and avoid overthinking.

3. Reframe Failure as Feedback

Treating failure as feedback shifts the focus from fear to learning, allowing you to grow from setbacks and refine your approach.

Example: After a project didn't go as planned, I reviewed what went wrong, noted lessons learned, and applied them to future tasks. This mindset reduced the fear of failure and encouraged continuous improvement.

4. Act Despite Uncertainty

Waiting for ideal conditions often leads to stagnation. Taking action in uncertain situations builds confidence and uncovers opportunities for growth.

Example: I stopped waiting for perfect conditions and set immediate, actionable goals. Each step forward, even without complete certainty, reinforced my ability to navigate challenges.

Reflection and Self-Monitoring

Weekly Reflection: "What actions did I take this week despite uncertainty, and how did they help me move forward?"

Monthly Reflection: "What lessons did I learn from challenges or failures this month, and how can I apply them to future efforts?"

Section 3

Mastering Relationships and Influence

Chapter 10

Becoming a Leader Before the Title

When I first began my career, I believed leadership was a reward—something granted after years of toil and a fancy title on your business card. The idea of leading without a title seemed foreign to me; I thought influence only came with authority. But over time, I realized that leadership isn't about what's on your business card—it's about how you show up, how you contribute, and how you inspire others, even when no one is watching. It's about taking initiative and making a positive impact, regardless of your position.

It's tempting to believe that leadership arrives with a promotion or a team to manage. But some of the most impactful leaders I've met led from the trenches—they influenced others without authority, earned trust through their actions, and inspired confidence long before any official recognition. They didn't wait for permission to lead; they saw opportunities to make a difference and seized them. These individuals understood that leadership is a choice, not a title.

Even Chad, with all his charisma and natural influence, stumbled here. He had the charm but sometimes missed the deeper essence of true leadership—a lesson I learned through my own journey. Chad often relied on his natural abilities to win people over, but leadership requires more than just charisma; it demands commitment, integrity, and a willingness to serve others. It's about being the person others can rely on when challenges arise.

Leading Without the Title

Most of us kick off our careers shoulder to shoulder with our peers, not above them. But even without a title, we face a choice: do we wait for instructions, or do we take the initiative and set the pace? The decision to lead isn't about authority; it's about attitude and the willingness to step forward.

Back when I was just an analyst among analysts, without any managerial title, I began to see that I could still influence how our team operated. I started to notice gaps in our processes, areas where we could improve efficiency or collaborate better. Instead of waiting for someone else to address them, I took action. I started volunteering to mentor new hires, running knowledge-sharing sessions, and stepping up whenever we hit a rough patch on a project.

By proactively contributing, I helped create a more cohesive and effective team environment. I wasn't trying to take over or tell others what to do; I simply saw areas where I could help and offered my support.

Soon enough, colleagues sought me out for advice—not because I was in charge, but because they trusted me to help them navigate challenges. They saw me as a resource, someone who could provide guidance and support when they needed it most. This not only benefited them but also allowed me to develop my own skills in communication, problem-solving, and leadership.

This subtle shift made a world of difference. Without a title, I was unknowingly cultivating leadership skills. So when the opportunity for a formal role arose, I had already demonstrated my capability. Leadership had become a part of who I was, not just a role I aspired to. It taught me that anyone can lead, regardless of their position.

The Myth of "When I'm in Charge..."

Many believe they'll step into leadership behaviors once they have the title, but leadership begins long before any promotion. Waiting for authority to lead is like waiting for permission to be yourself—it holds you back from reaching your full potential. The surest way to show you're ready for leadership is to lead where you are. Leadership is a practice, not a position, and the more you engage in it, the more natural it becomes.

A mentor once advised me, "If you want to be recognized as a leader, tackle the tasks others avoid." Those words resonated deeply. I realized that true leaders aren't afraid to step into the difficult situations, the ones that require courage and resilience. They see challenges as opportunities to grow and to demonstrate their commitment to the team's success.

So I began taking on the dreaded assignments—the messy projects, challenging clients, and those late-night emergencies. It wasn't glamorous. It was tough, often thankless work. But it taught me to manage under pressure, remain calm amidst chaos, and navigate the unpredictable.

I learned how to make decisions with limited information, how to rally a team when morale was low, and how to find solutions when none seemed apparent. These experiences were invaluable in shaping my leadership abilities.

Chad, meanwhile, often waited for formal authority before stepping up. Without a designated role, he'd sometimes hang back, missing opportunities to lead informally. It's not that he lacked the ability; he simply didn't perceive the value in leading without recognition. He believed that leadership was tied to status, not action. This mindset limited his growth and the impact he could have had.

But here's the catch: waiting for perfect conditions means missing real-time opportunities to hone leadership skills. Leadership is about stepping up, even when it's not mandated. It's about seeing a need and deciding to fill it, about influencing others through your actions and attitudes. The more you practice leading without authority, the more natural it becomes. It's an investment in yourself and in those around you.

Making an Impact Without Direct Control

Leading without authority means influencing without orders. It relies on persuasion, active listening, and relationship-building. It's about inspiring others to follow your lead because they want to, not because they have to. This form of leadership often requires a deeper understanding of people's motivations and how to align them with common goals.

I recall a tense period during a complex project. Conflicting directives from various departments left us gridlocked. Deadlines were approaching, and frustration was mounting. Though not the project lead, I saw the confusion stalling our progress. The team needed clarity, and waiting wasn't an option. I felt compelled to act, even if it meant stepping outside my usual responsibilities.

Rather than waiting passively, I took the initiative to gather all stakeholders for a meeting. I reached out to each department, emphasizing the importance of aligning our efforts. I outlined the challenges, offered potential solutions, and invited everyone to voice their concerns. By facilitating open communication, we were able to identify common goals and agree on a path forward.

It wasn't in my job description, but it cleared the air and realigned the team. This experience taught me that titles aren't prerequisites for creating clarity or resolving conflicts. Influence comes from your ability to bring people together and create a shared understanding, even when you're not in charge.

By stepping up, I was able to make a significant impact, and the project ultimately succeeded because of our collaborative efforts. It reinforced the idea that leadership is about serving the team and the mission.

Building Trust and Credibility

Leading without authority hinges on trust. Without it, even the best ideas fall flat. Building trust is a gradual process that requires consistency, transparency, and genuine concern for others.

While it's tempting to focus on impressing higher-ups, genuine influence grows from relationships with those around you. It's about being reliable, showing empathy, and demonstrating that you have the team's best interests at heart. People follow those they respect and believe in.

I learned this the hard way after attempting to implement a change without securing my peers' support. Believing I was acting in the project's best interest, I inadvertently alienated those whose support I needed most. My intentions were good, but my approach lacked collaboration.

It required sincere apologies and effort to rebuild trust, teaching me that leadership is less about directives and more about earning respect. I began involving others in decision-making, seeking their input, and valuing their perspectives. This not only improved our working relationships but also led to better outcomes, as we benefited from diverse ideas and collective wisdom.

The Takeaway

Leadership begins with a mindset, not a title. No matter where you are in the hierarchy, you can influence, guide, and foster trust and collaboration. Don't wait for permission. Step up, lean in, and watch your influence expand. By leading where you are, you not only enhance your own growth but also contribute to a culture of empowerment and excellence within your organization. Leadership is a journey, and it starts with the choices you make every day.

Action Plan: Leading Without a Title

Objective: Develop leadership skills through proactive actions, influence, and trust-building to demonstrate your capabilities, regardless of formal authority.

Framework: Follow the below framework to lead effectively, even without a formal title, by taking initiative, fostering collaboration, and building credibility.

1. Lead by Supporting Your Team

Leadership begins with small, consistent actions that build trust and show your commitment to the team's success. Supporting your peers lays the foundation for influence, even without formal authority.

Example: I mentored new hires, organized knowledge-sharing sessions, and stepped in during difficult moments. These efforts built trust and made me a resource the team relied on.

2. Volunteer for Challenging Tasks

Taking on tasks others avoid builds resilience, sharpens your problem-solving skills, and positions you as someone willing to take initiative.

Example: I volunteered for a high-pressure project no one else wanted, which taught me how to handle stress and earned me a reputation as someone who could tackle tough challenges.

3. Influence Through Communication, Not Authority

When you can't rely on formal power, clarity and collaboration are your strongest tools. Facilitating discussions and resolving conflicts demonstrate leadership in action.

Example: During a project with conflicting directives, I organized a meeting to clarify expectations, encouraged open discussion, and helped the team align. My initiative resolved confusion and demonstrated influence without authority.

4. Build Trust by Earning Respect

Trust is the foundation of leadership. It's earned through collaboration, follow-through, and consistently supporting others' success.

Example: Whenever I pushed a decision without consulting my peers, it has almost always led to resistance and strained relationships. Rebuilding trust taught me to involve others in decisions, prioritize collaboration, and show respect for their perspectives.

Reflection and Self-Monitoring

Weekly Reflection: "What actions did I take to support my team and demonstrate leadership this week?"

Monthly Reflection: "How effectively did I build trust and influence within my team? What steps can I take next month to strengthen these skills further?"

Chapter 11

The Art of Self-Promotion Without Bragging

Let's be honest: self-promotion often gets a bad rap. We picture someone endlessly bragging, turning every meeting into a "look at me" session. We've all met that person. And yes, Chad might have once brought donuts to the office just so he could casually mention that he single-handedly saved a project. It was hard not to roll our eyes, even as we enjoyed the treat. The fear of being perceived this way can make many of us shy away from promoting our achievements.

But here's the thing: self-promotion doesn't have to be cringeworthy. Done right, it's essential for ensuring your efforts are recognized and valued. In a competitive workplace, staying silent about your achievements can mean missed opportunities and unrecognized contributions. It's about finding the balance between humility and visibility. When you share your successes appropriately, you help others understand the value you bring.

The Fine Line Between Confidence and Bragging

I once believed that hard work spoke for itself. I thought if I just focused on delivering results, people would notice. But I observed that those who strategically shared their successes received more recognition. They weren't necessarily more skilled; they were simply better at highlighting their contributions. It wasn't about boasting; it was about confidently ensuring their work wasn't overlooked. They understood that visibility is a key component of career advancement.

This realization led me to understand that self-promotion is not about being loud; it's about being visible. It's about making sure that the right people are aware of the value you're adding to the organization. If you don't advocate for yourself, who will? By thoughtfully communicating your accomplishments, you position yourself for new opportunities and growth.

Framing the Story, Not the Spotlight

Effective self-promotion is about storytelling. Rather than proclaiming, "I did this amazing thing," frame it as, "Here's how we tackled a challenge and the impact it had." By focusing on the narrative and the results, you engage others and highlight your role within the bigger picture. This approach is more relatable and less likely to be perceived as self-centered.

For example, instead of "I saved the project," try, "Our team reduced turnaround by 20%, keeping us ahead of schedule. Here's what we learned that could help others." This approach shares credit, demonstrates leadership, and provides value to your audience. It transforms a self-centered statement into a collaborative success story. It also opens the door for others to learn from your experience. And who knows, you might even enjoy that donut without ulterior motives. People are more receptive to genuine sharing than to blatant self-promotion.

Learning from Chad: Knowing When to Share

Chad, ever the example, has a knack for sharing his achievements, though perhaps more directly than I prefer. He understands the importance of visibility, and he's aware that timing and context are crucial. By seizing casual opportunities to mention his successes, he ensures that key people are aware of his contributions.

While I might wait for formal settings, Chad casually mentions his successes in everyday conversations with leadership. "By the way, we just wrapped up that project 15% under budget," he'd mention with a grin. It wasn't about boasting; it was about ensuring key people were aware of his contributions. His confidence made an impression, but sometimes his approach lacked tact.

However, Chad sometimes missed the mark by not acknowledging how his self-promotion affected others. He'd highlight his successes but occasionally forget to credit the team. It wasn't that he didn't appreciate them; he just didn't always share the spotlight as generously as he could have. This oversight could create resentment and undermine his relationships with colleagues. It's important to remember that success is often a team effort.

Strategies for Smart Self-Promotion

So, how can you strike the balance? Here are strategies that worked for me:

- **Focus on Impact:** Highlight how your achievements benefited the team or organization. Instead of "I closed a big deal," say "We secured a new client, boosting our quarterly revenue by 15%." A subtle shift with significant impact. It shows you're contributing to larger goals. This makes your success relevant to others.

- **Share Credit Generously:** Recognize your team's efforts. This doesn't diminish your role; it enhances your leadership image. People value leaders who acknowledge others, building goodwill and fostering a positive work environment. It encourages collaboration and mutual support.

- **Choose the Right Moment:** Timing is key in sharing successes. Often, the ideal time is during one-on-ones, team debriefs, or project updates. Understand your audience and pick the appropriate moment. This ensures your message is received positively and doesn't come across as self-serving. Being considerate of others' time and context shows professionalism.

- **Keep a "Wins" Log:** Document your achievements regularly. It's helpful for self-reflection, performance reviews, and when asked, "What have you been working on?" You'll have concrete examples ready, avoiding last-minute scrambles. This also helps you track your progress and identify areas for growth. It's a valuable tool for career development.

- **Be Authentic:** Authenticity builds trust. Share your successes honestly, without exaggeration. People appreciate sincerity, and it strengthens your credibility. Authentic self-promotion resonates more and is more likely to be well-received. It shows integrity and humility.

Why Visibility Matters

This isn't about seeking praise; it's about aligning your work with company goals and ensuring its value is recognized. Too often, talented individuals remain unseen, missing out on opportunities. Highlighting your achievements positions you for growth and ensures your efforts contribute to the larger vision. Visibility allows you to demonstrate your potential and readiness for increased responsibilities.

And sometimes, it involves adopting Chad's intentionality in sharing your accomplishments, but with a touch more finesse. It's about recognizing your value, presenting it appropriately, and ensuring your work shines without overshadowing others. By being strategic without being self-aggrandizing, you build a reputation as a collaborative, effective professional. Your career advancement often depends on how well others understand and appreciate your contributions.

The Takeaway

Self-promotion can be collaborative. It's about ensuring your contributions are recognized and valued by those who matter. By focusing on your impact, sharing credit, and communicating authentically, it becomes less about bragging and more about sharing your value. Embrace self-promotion as a tool for growth, both for yourself and your organization. When done right, it enhances not only your career but also the success of those around you.

Action Plan: Mastering Self-Promotion with Humility

Objective: To promote your achievements authentically, ensuring recognition while fostering collaboration and impact..

Framework: Follow these steps to share your achievements effectively, ensuring your work is visible without coming across as boastful or self-centered.

1. Focus on Impact Over Ego

Emphasizing the broader impact of your work ensures others see its value while keeping the focus off self-praise.

Example: Instead of saying, "I closed the deal," highlight the result: "Our team's efforts brought in a new client, increasing quarterly revenue by 15%." This showcases your value in a team-oriented way.

2. Share Credit Generously

Recognizing the contributions of others reinforces your role as a collaborative leader and strengthens relationships.

Example: Rather than saying, "I led the project to success," say, "I collaborated with [specific team members] to achieve this outcome; their expertise was invaluable." Sharing credit builds goodwill and trust.

3. Time Your Wins Thoughtfully

Choosing the right moments to share your achievements ensures they feel relevant and natural, rather than forced.

Example: During a one-on-one meeting, I mentioned, "Last week, we improved turnaround time by 20%, which helped us meet the deadline," making it part of a progress update rather than self-promotion.

4. Keep a "Wins" Document

Tracking accomplishments makes it easier to share meaningful examples when the opportunity arises.

Example: Maintaining a list of completed projects, key metrics, and feedback helped me confidently articulate my contributions during performance reviews and impromptu discussions with leadership.

Reflection and Self-Monitoring

Weekly Reflection: "Did I effectively communicate my contributions this week in a way that felt authentic and team-focused?"

Monthly Reflection: "Have I maintained a balance between sharing my achievements and highlighting the team's efforts?"

Chapter 12

Creating Your Personal Brand

Believe it or not, you already have a personal brand. It's the impression you leave, the tone of your emails, the thoughts that arise when your name appears on a project. Every interaction, every piece of work contributes to how others perceive you. The question is: are you shaping it intentionally, or is it happening by default? Taking control of your personal brand can significantly influence your career trajectory.

Initially, I didn't consider my "brand" at all. I assumed only influencers or entrepreneurs needed to think about that. But as I climbed the ladder, I noticed some people had reputations that spoke volumes before they even entered a room. They were the experts, the "fixers," the creative problem-solvers everyone sought out. They were known, respected, and in demand. Their brands preceded them and opened doors.

Then there was Chad, whose brand was, well, a bit more colorful. He was famous for his confidence, his knack for charming anyone, and his ability to delegate most tasks yet still appear heroic. Sure, his methods sometimes backfired, but Chad grasped a vital lesson I took longer to learn: your reputation is your brand—one of your most potent assets. Understanding and cultivating it can significantly impact your career progression and opportunities.

What Do You Want to Be Known For?

The first step in building your personal brand is defining what you want to be known for. Are you the punctual project deliverer? The creative thinker? The go-to mentor? Your brand should reflect your strengths, passions, and the value you bring to the organization. It's about identifying your unique selling proposition.

I chose to be the go-to expert in data, integration, and analytics—the one people consult about industry trends or complex data-driven business problems. I aimed to be seen as someone who could find the answers, even if I didn't have them immediately. This meant continuously developing my skills, staying updated on industry developments, and being proactive in sharing knowledge. I wanted to be a trusted resource.

Finding answers doesn't mean knowing everything—it means leveraging your network. With a robust, diverse network, there's always someone who can help or connect you to the right person. By being the connector, I added value not just through my expertise but also through facilitating solutions. It's about connecting the dots, even if those dots aren't yours. This approach enhances your brand as a collaborative and resourceful professional.

Why You Need an Elevator Pitch

Now, let's discuss an underrated branding tool: the elevator pitch. An elevator pitch is a brief summary of who you are, what you do, and the value you offer—deliverable in the span of an elevator ride. Simple in concept, immense in power. It can be a game-changer in making strong first impressions. Its goal isn't to state your job title but to convey what sets you apart.

Advantages of an Elevator Pitch:

- **Clarity:** Distills your role and its significance into a few sentences.
- **Visibility:** Leaves a memorable impression on leadership or new colleagues.
- **Opportunity:** Sparks curiosity, inviting follow-up questions that can open doors.
- **Confidence**: Helps you articulate your value clearly and concisely, boosting self-assurance in professional interactions.
- **Efficiency**: Enables you to communicate your expertise effectively in time-sensitive situations.

Examples of Good and Bad Elevator Pitches:

- **Bad Pitch:** "I work in marketing, handling social media and emails." True, but generic and forgettable. It lacks impact and doesn't show why it matters.
- **Good Pitch:** "I boost brands' online presence with targeted social media strategies. Recently, I led a campaign increasing followers by 30% in three months." Focuses on impact, clear and concise, showcasing value. It invites the listener to view you as a problem-solver they might need. It makes you memorable.

The Risk of Working in a Silo

Early in my career, I mistakenly believed that doing good work was enough to be noticed. I toiled diligently but didn't share my results beyond my immediate team. I wasn't showcasing the value I brought. Opportunities slipped by, and I realized I was invisible to the broader organization. My contributions were confined to a small circle.

Working in a silo is detrimental to career growth. You might excel at your job, but if others aren't aware, your brand lacks influence. Hidden efforts lead to missed growth opportunities. Invisibility means your brand doesn't extend beyond your circle. Without a broader brand, you lack organizational influence.

And here's where Chad (yes, Chad again) provides a valuable counterpoint. Chad was never shy about sharing his accomplishments, but he also knew how to do it strategically—something we talked about back in our prior chapter on Self-Promotion. While I was focusing on just getting the work done, he was making sure that people at every level knew the value he was bringing. Sure, sometimes he overdid it, and not every self-promotion attempt was met with enthusiasm, but he made sure he wasn't invisible. Chad's approach might have lacked finesse at times, but he got one thing right: if you're not talking about your contributions, you're not building a reputation outside your own bubble.

Chad built relationships across departments, and people knew what he stood for. His brand was widespread. Despite occasional missteps, he understood that not sharing your contributions limits your reputation. His example taught me that staying silent about your achievements can keep you stuck in the shadows, missing out on opportunities to grow and influence.

Building Your Brand Through Actions

After defining your brand, consistent actions must support it. It's insufficient to label yourself without acting differently. Brand building is a long-term commitment to consistency.

Your brand evolves with your career growth, shifting interests, and industry changes. Initially, I wanted to be known as the guy who could execute any project, regardless of challenges. But as I transitioned into strategic roles, my focus shifted. I aimed to be seen as a strategic thinker, someone who could not only deliver but also innovate and lead.

This meant taking on projects that stretched my abilities, seeking leadership opportunities, and continuously learning. I began sharing thought leadership pieces, mentoring others, and contributing to strategic discussions. By aligning my actions with my evolving brand, I reinforced my reputation and opened doors to new opportunities. It demonstrated my growth and adaptability.

Consistency doesn't mean rigidity. It's about staying true to your core values while adapting to new roles and challenges. Your brand should be a reflection of who you are and who you aspire to be, guided by purposeful actions. It's about authenticity and intentionality.

The Takeaway

Your personal brand is defined by your actions, not just your words. It's built through consistent effort, nurtured relationships, and the value you add. If you're hidden away, step out and ensure your efforts are visible to key people. Because excellence without visibility means missed opportunities.

While Chad may rely on charm, lasting influence stems from authenticity and reliability built over time. By intentionally shaping

The Lost Map To Your Career

your brand, you take control of your professional narrative. Invest in yourself, communicate your value, and let your actions speak loudly. In doing so, you not only advance your career but also contribute meaningfully to your organization and those around you. Your personal brand is a powerful tool—use it wisely.

Action Plan: Building Your Personal Brand

Objective: To shape a personal brand that highlights your strengths, aligns with your values, and ensures your contributions are visible and impactful.

Framework: These steps below will help you intentionally develop and maintain a personal brand that reflects your expertise, reinforces your reputation, and adapts to your career growth.

1. Define What You Want to Be Known For

Establishing a clear focus for your personal brand ensures you are top of mind when specific challenges or opportunities arise.

Example: I decided to be recognized as the go-to expert in data analytics and problem-solving. I built my expertise and ensured my name was associated with solving complex data challenges.

2. Craft a Memorable Elevator Pitch

A well-crafted elevator pitch makes your role and value clear while leaving a lasting impression.

Example: Instead of saying, "I work in data," I began saying, "I help companies make smarter decisions by turning complex data into actionable insights," which created curiosity and highlighted my expertise.

3. Step Out of Your Silo

Sharing your accomplishments beyond your immediate team builds visibility and expands your influence.

Example: I started presenting project outcomes in meetings with cross-functional teams, ensuring my contributions were known beyond my direct circle.

4. Build Your Brand Through Consistent Actions

Aligning your actions with your desired brand ensures authenticity and strengthens your reputation over time.

Example: To reinforce my brand as a problem-solver, I consistently delivered on complex projects and took on challenging tasks that highlighted my expertise.

5. Adapt Your Brand as You Grow

Evolving your brand to match your career trajectory ensures it remains relevant and aligned with your goals.

Example: As I transitioned from execution-focused roles to leadership, I shifted my brand toward strategic thinking by taking on initiatives that aligned with organizational goals.

Reflection and Self-Monitoring

Weekly Reflection: "What actions did I take this week to reinforce my desired personal brand?"

Monthly Reflection: "How has my personal brand evolved, and does it align with my current goals and career aspirations?"

Chapter 13

Voicing Concerns and Tackling Conflict

Every professional journey reaches a crossroads where you must choose between raising your voice or biting your tongue. For some of us, it happens early—when a manager makes a decision that feels completely wrong, or a colleague's behavior starts causing friction in the team. For others, it comes later—when you've been through enough projects to know that silence isn't always golden and can sometimes be a ticking time bomb.

For me, the decision to voice my concerns came after a series of frustrating incidents. I had a manager who, quite frankly, didn't have a clue. He would ask me to send emails that didn't make sense, offer directions so vague I felt like I needed a treasure map to find the point, and often ignore major red flags in our projects. At first, I thought it was just me—that maybe I wasn't seeing the bigger picture, or that he had some master plan I just didn't understand.

"Maybe I'm missing something," I'd think, second-guessing my own instincts.

But as time went on, the frustration built. Every day, I'd sit through meetings where I knew we were headed in the wrong direction, but I said nothing. I didn't want to rock the boat. I didn't want to be seen as the difficult one. So, I kept quiet. And the more I stayed quiet, the worse the situation became. It was like watching a slow-motion train wreck, powerless to stop it.

When Silence Becomes Harmful

The problem with not speaking up is that, eventually, it starts to affect not just you, but the entire team. When no one voices concerns, bad decisions go unchecked, and small issues snowball into bigger problems. That's what happened in my case. Projects started missing deadlines, the team's morale took a hit, and leadership still had no idea what was wrong.

One day, after my boss had asked me to send yet another ill-advised email, I snapped. "This doesn't feel right," I told him. It was the first time I had ever spoken up directly. And while I won't say the conversation went smoothly, it was the first step in realizing that voicing concerns—no matter how uncomfortable—is necessary for the health of any team. It felt like a weight lifted off my shoulders, even though the air was thick with tension.

Choosing the Right Time and Place

Of course, there's a right way and a wrong way to voice concerns. Timing is everything. You don't want to interrupt a meeting with a barrage of criticism or publicly call someone out in front of others. That's a fast track to creating unnecessary tension.

Instead, find a private moment to have a candid conversation. Frame your concerns in a constructive way. Instead of saying, "This project is doomed," try something like, "I've noticed a few risks that could impact our progress—can we discuss them?" It's all about the delivery. No one likes a complainer, but everyone appreciates someone who raises concerns with solutions in mind. I found that pulling my boss aside after a meeting led to more productive discussions.

When (Over)Confidence Meets Consequences

Even Chad wasn't immune to the pitfalls of silence. I remember a time when he faced a particularly challenging project. It was one of those high-visibility assignments where everyone's eyes were on the deliverables. Chad, as always, carried himself with his signature confidence, thinking he could handle the hurdles as they came. He chose to keep the issues to himself, believing he'd sort them out before they became a problem.

But this time, things didn't go according to plan. Critical information from another department was delayed, and without raising a red flag early, Chad's project slipped further and further behind. By the time he finally brought up the delays to leadership, it was too late to adjust timelines, and the project missed a crucial deadline.

It was a rare stumble for Chad, but an important one. He learned that sometimes, no amount of charm or confidence can substitute for clear communication. If he'd spoken up earlier, management could have helped him navigate the delay. But by choosing silence, he missed the chance to get the support he needed. Even the most self-assured among us can trip when we walk alone.

The lesson? No matter how confident you are, trying to handle everything on your own can backfire. Sometimes, it's not just about showing strength—it's about showing transparency.

Handling Conflict with Peers

Conflict isn't just limited to management. Sometimes, it's your peers or direct reports causing friction. I've been on both sides of the equation, and neither one is easy. But here's the thing: avoiding conflict doesn't make it go away. In fact, it usually makes it worse.

I remember a time when two team members on a project I was leading simply couldn't get along. They were constantly butting heads, and it was affecting the entire team's productivity. I tried to ignore it at first, hoping they'd work it out on their own, but it only got worse. Finally, I had to step in and mediate.

The key to resolving conflict is addressing it head-on, but with empathy. Don't just wade into the middle of a fight and start taking sides. Instead, listen to both perspectives, acknowledge the issues, and work together to find common ground. People often just want to be heard, and giving them the chance to voice their frustrations can go a long way in defusing a situation. After a lengthy discussion, not only did they resolve their issues, but they also developed a newfound respect for each other.

When to Escalate

Sometimes, despite your best efforts, a conflict or issue can't be resolved on your own. This is where knowing when to escalate is critical. There's no shame in bringing an issue to higher leadership if it's affecting your ability to do your job or damaging the team dynamic. The trick is to do it professionally and with all the facts in hand.

When I finally had to go above my manager's head, I didn't just march into the office and rant. I came with data, examples, and specific suggestions for how things could improve. By framing the conversation around solutions rather than complaints, I was able to get the support I needed to fix the underlying issues.

Chad's experience taught me that even the most confident among us need to ask for help sometimes. It's not about admitting defeat; it's about ensuring that the project and the team succeed. Sometimes, the strongest move is recognizing you can't do it alone.

The Takeaway

Voicing concerns and tackling conflict isn't easy, but it's essential if you want to grow and lead effectively. Silence may feel like the safer option in the short term, but in the long term, it creates bigger problems for you and your team. Learn to speak up when necessary, choose your battles wisely, and remember—conflict isn't always a bad thing. When handled correctly, it can lead to growth, stronger teams, and better outcomes. Embrace the discomfort; it might just be the catalyst for positive change.

Action Plan: Handling Conflict and Voicing Concerns Effectively

Objective: To address conflicts and raise concerns constructively, fostering stronger team dynamics and achieving better outcomes.

Framework: These steps below will help you approach conflicts and concerns in a solution-oriented manner, enabling you to resolve issues early, maintain positive relationships, and promote a collaborative work environment.

1. Recognize When Silence is Harmful

Staying silent can allow problems to grow unchecked, delaying resolutions and exacerbating tensions. Acknowledging this is the first step toward proactive action.

Example: Addressing a manager's ineffective decisions improved team dynamics after silence had caused frustration. Proactively voicing concerns helps redirect efforts and enhance outcomes.

2. Choose the Right Time and Approach

Timing and delivery are crucial for addressing sensitive issues effectively. Framing concerns constructively encourages collaboration and receptiveness.

Example: Waiting for a private moment to discuss a tense issue allowed for a calmer, solution-focused conversation, leading to a more productive outcome than confronting it during a heated meeting.

3. Handle Peer Conflicts Head-On with Empathy

Avoiding conflicts among peers can worsen tensions and hinder teamwork. Directly addressing disputes while showing understanding helps resolve issues and rebuild collaboration.

Example: Mediating a clash between team members by listening to both sides and guiding them toward a shared solution strengthened their partnership and improved team cohesion.

4. Know When to Escalate

Some conflicts require leadership intervention. Escalating issues with specific examples and proposed solutions ensures that concerns are addressed constructively without harming relationships.

Example: Presenting data and actionable solutions while escalating a management issue led to leadership support and resolution, improving the team's working environment.

5. Embrace Transparency When Facing Challenges

Being transparent about challenges fosters trust and encourages collaborative problem-solving, preventing issues from escalating.

Example: Sharing a challenge with the team early allowed them to contribute solutions, preventing the issue from becoming more significant and reinforcing a culture of trust.

Reflection and Self-Monitoring

Weekly Reflection: "Did I address conflicts or concerns constructively this week? How did my approach impact team dynamics and outcomes?"

Monthly Reflection: "Have I fostered a culture of openness and transparency in handling conflicts? What could I improve in my approach to resolving concerns?"

Chapter 14

Asking for Help – Leveraging Your Network

For the longest time, asking for help felt like admitting I couldn't cut it on my own. I believed that asking for help meant I wasn't competent enough, that I couldn't hack it. It was like a sign saying, "I don't know what I'm doing." But here's the thing: not asking for help when you need it is like refusing to ask for directions when you're lost—it doesn't make you look smarter, it just makes the journey longer and more frustrating.

And trust me, Chad never hesitated to ask for help. The man practically had a degree in delegating. I'd watch as he effortlessly asked for input, called on connections, and somehow, no matter the task, there'd be a group of people swooping in to assist him. Meanwhile, I was drowning in work because I was too stubborn (or maybe too proud) to say, "I could really use a hand with this."

It took a few career bumps—and missed deadlines—before I realized that Chad had it right. Asking for help isn't a weakness. In fact, it's the opposite. It's one of the smartest things you can do, provided you're asking the right people, in the right way.

Why We Struggle to Ask for Help

Let's get this out of the way: There's an illusion that asking for help makes you look weak, incapable, or dependent. I thought that too. But the reality is, nobody gets anywhere entirely on their own. Behind every successful leader is a network of mentors, peers, and experts they've leaned on to guide them. Even the most "self-made" person you know has asked for help at some point.

In fact, people often respect you more for knowing when to reach out. It shows that you're smart enough to recognize the gaps in your knowledge or capacity and are taking proactive steps to solve the problem. It's like that one kid in school who always raised their hand with a question—sure, some people rolled their eyes, but guess who probably aced the test?

Building and Leveraging Your Network

Here's the catch, though: asking for help works best when you've built a strong network to ask. It's not about running to anyone and everyone for assistance—it's about knowing who to approach for specific needs. Think of your network like a toolkit. You wouldn't use a hammer to fix a broken circuit (unless you're Chad, who once thought he could solve every office issue by "hitting refresh"). You need to know which tool to pull out for which job.

So, how do you build that network?

- **Nurture relationships:** Your network isn't just the people you meet at a conference and never speak to again. It's the colleagues you mentor, the peers you've collaborated with, the industry experts you've connected with over time. Relationships need to be nurtured; you can't expect someone to help you if you haven't invested any time in the relationship. It's like tending a garden—you have to water it regularly to see it flourish.

- **Give before you ask:** The best networks are built on reciprocity. If you're always the one taking and never giving, people will eventually stop answering your calls. But if you're the kind of person who helps others when they're in need, they'll be more inclined to return the favor when you're the one asking. Think of it as depositing goodwill into a bank—you can't withdraw what you haven't put in.

- **Diversify your network:** Just as you shouldn't rely on one skill for your entire career, you shouldn't rely on just one type of person in your network. Diversify. You need people with different expertise, from different departments, and even different industries. That way, when you encounter a problem, you have multiple people you can turn to for advice.

How to Ask for Help Effectively

Now, once you've built that network, how do you ask for help in a way that doesn't feel awkward or burdensome? Here's the secret: Be clear, be concise, and offer solutions, not just problems.

Instead of saying, "I'm stuck on this project, what should I do?"—which leaves the person guessing at what the problem even is—try, "I'm working on the project deliverable, and I've noticed some inconsistencies in the data. I've tried A and B, but I'm still seeing gaps in communication. Do you have any suggestions based on your experience?"

This approach does two things:

1. It shows that you've already put in the effort to solve the problem yourself, which demonstrates initiative.

2. It gives the person clear context, so they're more likely to offer helpful advice without feeling like you're offloading all your work onto them.

Also, don't just approach someone when you're in crisis mode. If you've been maintaining your relationships (remember, networks aren't built overnight), you can ask for input and advice before a situation becomes critical. It's much easier for someone to help you if you're proactive, rather than waiting until you're drowning. Think of it as regular maintenance rather than emergency repair.

The Chad Strategy (With a Twist)

As much as I hate to admit it, Chad's been onto something all along. He's always leveraged his network—whether by borrowing someone's expertise or pulling in a favor—and he's done so with ease. But where Chad occasionally stumbled was not always giving back in return. It's one thing to know how to ask for help; it's another to make sure the relationship remains balanced.

So, be like Chad... but maybe with a bit more self-awareness. Don't hesitate to reach out when you need help, but also keep an eye on how you can be the person offering help as well. The best networks are those that flow both ways. It's about creating a symbiotic relationship where everyone benefits.

The Takeaway

Asking for help doesn't make you less capable; it makes you resourceful. It shows that you're willing to learn, grow, and tackle problems head-on, rather than letting your ego get in the way. And remember, your network is there for a reason—don't let it go to waste. Whether it's solving a team coordination issue or seeking advice on how to handle a tricky office situation, leverage the people around you.

Even if Chad might sometimes seem like he's asking for help to avoid work, there's a valuable lesson in how he uses his network. The key difference? Make sure you're contributing back to the people who help you. Asking for help is part of career growth, and the sooner you embrace it, the faster you'll move forward. After all, no one climbs a mountain alone.

Action Plan: Effectively Asking for Help and Leveraging Your Network

Objective: To cultivate a supportive network, approach help-seeking strategically, and foster mutually beneficial relationships that enhance personal and professional growth.

Framework: These steps below will help you ask for help effectively and build a balanced, mutually beneficial network by reframing help-seeking as a strength, maintaining diverse connections, and fostering reciprocal relationships.

1. Reframe Asking for Help as a Strength

Asking for help is a proactive way to learn from others, gain new perspectives, and accelerate personal growth. Viewing it as resourcefulness rather than weakness encourages openness and collaboration.

Example: When seeking advice, remind yourself that it demonstrates a commitment to improvement. Reaching out to others for their expertise strengthens both individual and collective results.

2. Build and Maintain a Diverse Network

A well-rounded network offers varied perspectives and support across different areas of professional and personal growth. Actively engaging with colleagues, peers, and mentors fosters a reliable set of connections.

Example: Regularly nurture relationships by checking in with connections through messages, calls, or casual meet-ups. Include individuals from different departments, industries, or expertise levels to diversify your network.

3. Offer Help Before You Ask for It

Building goodwill by offering assistance to others strengthens trust and creates a foundation for reciprocal support when you need it.
Example: Look for opportunities to contribute to others' success, such as sharing resources, providing feedback, or assisting on a project. These actions encourage balanced and mutually beneficial relationships.

4. Be Clear and Concise When Asking for Help

Providing clear context and actionable steps when seeking help makes it easier for others to provide meaningful support. Vague requests can lead to confusion and missed opportunities for collaboration.

Example: Frame your request with context, specific needs, and steps already taken. For example, say, "I'm deciding between two strategies for this project and would value your input on which aligns best with our goals."

5. Keep Track of Contributions and Offer Support in Return

Fostering a strong network requires reciprocation and recognition of others' efforts. Following up with those who've supported you and offering your assistance builds lasting, dependable relationships.

Example: After receiving help, reach out to express gratitude and offer your support in return. This approach reinforces trust and ensures the relationship remains mutually beneficial over time.

Reflection and Self-Monitoring

Weekly Reflection: "What steps did I take to build or maintain connections this week? How effectively did I ask for or offer help?"

Monthly Reflection: "Are my relationships within my network balanced and mutually beneficial? What can I do to strengthen them further?"

Chapter 15

Finding Mentors and Becoming One

If there's one thing that can significantly fast-track your career, it's having a mentor. I'm not talking about the kind of mentorship where someone offers vague advice like, "Work hard, and good things will come." I mean a mentor who can give you real, actionable guidance, tell you when you're screwing up, and show you how to fix it.

Of course, I learned this the hard way. Early in my career, I figured I could figure it all out on my own. I didn't think I needed a mentor because, well, I had Google. But Google can't give you advice that's tailored to your unique situation. It can't say, "Hey, maybe don't send that email when you're angry at 3 a.m." Or, "Here's how to navigate that tricky meeting with your boss without looking defensive."

Meanwhile, there was Chad again, making it look easy. He always had a mentor or two in his back pocket—senior leaders who vouched for him, gave him inside advice, and even provided him with opportunities that weren't available to the rest of us. At first, I thought Chad's mentors were just doing him favors because he was charismatic, but then I realized Chad was actually pretty good at choosing the right people to guide him. He knew that the right mentor could make all the difference. It wasn't just luck; it was strategy.

The Power of a Good Mentor

Finding the right mentor can feel like finding a needle in a haystack, especially if you're not sure what you're looking for. But when you do find one, it can be a game-changer. A good mentor provides more than just career advice—they offer perspective. They've been through the trenches, made their own mistakes, and can help you avoid making the same ones.

But here's the thing: Not every successful person is the right mentor for you. Just because someone has achieved great things in their career doesn't mean they'll be the best guide for your journey. The right mentor is someone who understands your strengths, sees where you need improvement, and has walked a similar path toward the goals you're aiming for. A mentor who comes from a similar background can relate to the challenges you face, but it's not mandatory. Often, the best mentorship comes from a combination of perspectives.

Ideally, you should have a few mentors to provide a well-rounded view:

- Someone from your background who understands the specifics of your role or industry.
- Someone outside your background but in the same industry, who can offer a fresh perspective on challenges.
- People who can open doors—mentors who have connections and can introduce you to new opportunities and expand your network.

Different mentors can offer different types of guidance, and successful people can have perspectives that are complete 180s of each other. Everyone's path to success is unique, shaped by their personality, experiences, and opportunities. Your job is to find the mentors whose advice resonates with you and feels like the best fit for your own journey. You don't have to—and shouldn't—take everyone's advice. If you try to follow every piece of guidance, you'll end up running in circles. Instead, trust your instincts and do what's best for you.

How to Find a Mentor

So, how do you actually go about finding a mentor? It's not as easy as walking up to someone you admire and saying, "Hey, will you be my mentor?" It's a bit more nuanced than that, but not as intimidating as it might seem.

- **Look for a Mentor, Not a Savior:** A mentor isn't there to fix your problems or take your burdens off your shoulders. They're there to guide you, offer perspective, and share their experience. You're still the one doing the work.

- **Identify What You Need:** Think about what you're looking for in a mentor. Do you need help with strategic thinking? Do you want someone who can help you navigate office politics? Or maybe you're looking for someone who has skills you want to develop. Being clear on what you're seeking will help you identify the right person.

- **Make It a Two-Way Street:** When you're asking someone to be your mentor, you're asking for a piece of their valuable time. And time, especially for busy professionals, is a precious resource. One of the best ways to approach a potential mentor is to show how you can add value to their journey as well. For example, if they're working on leading a practice of AI engineers and you have experience in that area, you could offer to help them upskill their team over the next six months. This turns your mentorship into a two-way partnership where both sides benefit.

Understanding what motivates your mentor professionally can help you tailor your offer. It could be a skill you bring to the table, a perspective they appreciate, or simply helping them achieve their goals in some way. This approach not only makes the ask feel less one-sided but also strengthens the bond, building a foundation of mutual respect and trust. And it ties back to building that upward network we talked about earlier—when you invest in helping others reach their goals, they're more inclined to help you reach yours.

- **Build a Relationship First:** Mentorship is built on trust and rapport, and that doesn't happen overnight. Start by engaging with the person—ask them for advice on a specific issue, compliment their work, or even offer to help them on a project. Let the relationship develop naturally before asking for a more formal mentorship.

- **Be Open to Unconventional Mentors:** Sometimes, the best mentors aren't the most obvious ones. They might not even be in your industry. I've learned just as much from peers and people at the same level as me as I have from senior leaders. Keep an open mind. Wisdom can come from the most unexpected places.

Mentorship Gone Wrong: Learning When to Walk Away

Not every mentorship experience is going to be a perfect fit, and sometimes, that's part of the learning process. While a good mentor can accelerate your growth, a mismatched one can hold you back—or even push you in the wrong direction. I've had my share of mentors who, with the best of intentions, ended up being more of a challenge than a benefit.

Take one of my early mentors, for example. He was a high-level executive, the kind of person whose office door you'd knock on with a sense of awe. I thought he'd be able to teach me everything I needed to know about navigating leadership. But as our mentorship progressed, I started to notice a disconnect. His advice often boiled down to, "Just make the tough calls and don't worry about the people who get in your way."

For him, it made sense—he was in a role where he had to make quick decisions and didn't have time to get caught up in the details. But I wasn't leading a division; I was managing a small team. What I needed was guidance on how to navigate the complex dynamics of getting my team on board with new projects, not a crash course in wielding authority. I realized that his perspective, while valuable in its own right, didn't align with the challenges I was facing.

At first, I tried to force myself to adopt his style, thinking that maybe I just needed to "toughen up." But it quickly became clear that it wasn't me—it was the fit. His advice was coming from a place of good intentions, but it wasn't what I needed at that stage of my career. So, I made the difficult decision to let go of that formal mentorship, while still respecting him as a leader.

And then there was Chad's experience. Chad had a mentor who believed that relationships were everything, that the way to move up was to network, network, and network some more. Chad took this advice to heart, spending more time building connections than actually getting the work done. It turned out that while relationships matter, so does delivering on your commitments. His mentor's advice, while great for someone in a sales role, didn't translate well into Chad's more operational role. Eventually, Chad realized that he had been so focused on building rapport that he was losing sight of what he was actually supposed to deliver.

These experiences taught us both an important lesson: not every mentor is right for every phase of your career, and sometimes, a mentor's advice might be better suited for a different path altogether. It's okay to recognize when a mentorship isn't working and to shift your focus. The best mentors guide you in a way that aligns with your strengths and your vision, not theirs.

The Takeaway

Mentorship isn't a magic wand, but it is a powerful tool. The right mentor can help you see things from a new perspective, guide you through tough times, and push you to reach your potential. And when you get to a place where you can do the same for others, it's even more rewarding.

So, don't be afraid to reach out for guidance, and don't hesitate to extend a hand to those coming up behind you. The best careers are built on a foundation of shared wisdom, and there's no shame in seeking (or giving) a little help along the way. Just remember, the goal isn't to find a mentor who will do the work for you—it's to find a group of people whose insights align with your path, and to choose the advice that truly fits your journey. In the end, mentorship is a two-way street paved with mutual growth.

Action Plan: Finding the Right Mentors and Becoming One

Objective: To effectively seek mentorship for personal growth while providing meaningful guidance to others, creating a cycle of mutual development.

Framework: A successful mentorship dynamic is built on clarity, mutual respect, and adaptability. Identifying mentors with relevant expertise, building genuine connections, and offering value in return ensures productive relationships. Similarly, transitioning to mentorship allows professionals to share knowledge and refine their leadership skills.

1. Identify What You Need in a Mentor

Mentorship is most effective when tailored to specific challenges, such as strategic thinking, team dynamics, or industry expertise. Reflecting on personal goals helps in finding mentors whose skills align with those needs.

Example: Evaluate areas where guidance is needed, such as leadership, technical skills, or career planning. Focused self-assessment ensures the mentor chosen can provide relevant support.

2. Build Relationships First

Strong mentorship relationships often develop naturally from existing connections. Engaging with potential mentors through casual interactions or collaborative efforts lays the foundation for deeper guidance.

Example: Approach potential mentors with curiosity by seeking advice on a specific issue or offering feedback on their work. This fosters trust and creates a pathway for a mentorship relationship to develop organically.

3. Make Mentorship a Two-Way Street

Effective mentorship involves reciprocity, where mentees contribute to their mentor's goals, creating a relationship based on mutual respect and shared value.

Example: Support the mentor's goals by offering assistance in areas of expertise or providing insights that complement their work. A reciprocal dynamic strengthens the relationship and enhances its benefits for both parties.

4. Recognize When Mentorship Isn't the Right Fit

Mentorship should evolve as needs and goals change. Regular evaluation ensures the guidance provided aligns with the mentee's current path and objectives.

Example: Periodically assess the mentorship relationship. If the advice no longer aligns with personal challenges or goals, consider seeking additional perspectives. Adaptability ensures mentorship remains relevant and effective.

5. Become a Mentor When You're Ready

Mentorship provides an opportunity to give back while reinforcing leadership and strategic thinking skills. Supporting others' growth creates a positive cycle of shared learning.

Example: Take on mentorship opportunities by guiding less experienced colleagues or peers. Sharing knowledge and lessons learned strengthens personal leadership abilities while contributing to the growth of others.

Reflection and Self-Monitoring

Weekly Reflection: "Did I take a meaningful step this week to strengthen a mentorship relationship or offer guidance to others?"

Monthly Reflection: "How have my mentorship relationships evolved this month? Am I providing or receiving value aligned with current goals?"

Chapter 16

Building Influence in a Remote/Hybrid World

The rise of remote and hybrid work environments has changed a lot about how we navigate our careers. Suddenly, that spontaneous chat at the coffee machine has been replaced by scheduled Zoom calls, and those casual hallway conversations with leadership? Well, now they're buried beneath a calendar of back-to-back meetings. And if you're like me, it sometimes feels like you're talking to a bunch of floating heads. How do you make yourself known and, more importantly, build influence when you're not in the room?

Back in the day, being visible at work meant literally being seen—showing up early, staying late, and making sure your contributions were noticed. It was those little things, like dropping into your manager's office with a quick update or making a passing comment during a team lunch that would plant the seeds of visibility. I remember one time a casual conversation about weekend plans with my boss ended up turning into a discussion about an upcoming project. It wasn't planned, but it helped put my name in the hat for more responsibilities.

But in a remote or hybrid world, visibility takes on a new meaning. It's not just about showing up on a video call; it's about making sure that, even from a distance, people know who you are, what you're contributing, and why you matter to the team. Now, instead of swinging by your boss's office, you might find yourself sending that Slack message that says, "Hey, just a heads up on the project status…" or chiming in during a meeting with, "I've got a thought on that."

The Struggle for Presence

When the pandemic first hit, I thought remote work would be a breeze. No commute, more flexibility, and hey, I'd get to avoid the small talk at the office. But what I didn't anticipate was how easy it was to become invisible. When you're not physically in the office, you miss out on those small moments—like when Chad used to bump into leadership while microwaving his lunch (though, in fairness, he once tried to microwave a burrito in tinfoil, which led to a spectacular fire alarm incident).

In the new normal of endless emails and virtual meetings, it was easy to feel disconnected. There's a big difference between casually running into your manager at the breakroom and trying to convey your ideas through a screen, where everyone is muted, and it's anyone's guess who will speak next. The spontaneous side conversations, the quick debriefs after a meeting—these all felt like things of the past. But while I struggled to adjust, I realized something crucial: influence in a remote world doesn't just happen. You have to be intentional about it. You have to create the moments of connection that used to happen by chance.

If the best way to predict the future is to create it, then in a hybrid world, the best way to build influence is to create opportunities for interaction—whether that's a well-timed email update or a thoughtfully prepared comment in a meeting that makes leadership perk up.

Creating Your Own Visibility

If you think that just doing great work is enough to get noticed, remote work will set you straight fast. When you're not in the office, it's easier for your contributions to get overlooked. So, how do you make sure your work doesn't go unseen? It's all about being proactive.

For example, one of the best habits I picked up was sending a weekly email update to my manager. It wasn't just a list of tasks I'd completed, but a summary of how those tasks moved our larger goals forward. "This week, I finalized the data report that will help the sales team target our key markets—expect a 5% bump in conversion next quarter." It wasn't showboating; it was making sure that even if I wasn't seen, my impact was.

And yes, that means sometimes you'll have to toot your own horn a little—just don't blow a trumpet in their faces. It's a balance. Think of it as sharing your accomplishments, not boasting about them. If Chad can send an email with five exclamation points about finishing his timesheet on time, you can certainly share the project wins that actually matter.

Leveraging the Digital Water Cooler

You might think the days of water cooler conversations are over, but they've just moved online. Whether it's through team chat channels, virtual happy hours, or even those icebreaker questions that make everyone roll their eyes, these are your new opportunities to connect.

It may seem trivial, but those little interactions can go a long way in building rapport. Drop a quick message to a colleague congratulating them on a job well done, or share an interesting article related to your industry in the team chat. Not only does it show that you're engaged, but it also keeps you in the loop of what's going on beyond your own projects. Plus, it's a good way to show that you're not just a talking head on a screen—you're a person who cares about the team's success.

Humanizing Remote Interactions

One of my mentors once shared a simple but profound truth: every person we work with brings their own personal baggage to the table. They carry stories of joy, stress, or heartache—things we might never see, and frankly, things that aren't always our business. Yet, these experiences shape how they show up at work and how they interact with us.

In a remote environment, we often lose touch with this human side of our colleagues. We become just voices on a call, boxes on a screen, disconnected from the subtleties of a smile or a frown. Many of the best leaders I've worked with understood this and made it a point to humanize our interactions. They'd spend the first 5-10 minutes of meetings chatting about life—weekend plans, a new hobby, or how the kids were doing—before diving into business.

Those small moments of connection matter. They're not just about filling time; they're about showing that you care about the person behind the job title. It builds a sense of mutual loyalty and helps create a positive work environment, even from a distance. Sometimes, a quick conversation about your favorite TV show or a shared laugh about the latest viral meme is the bridge that turns a colleague into a teammate, making all the difference in how you work together.

Mastering the Art of Virtual Presence

In a remote or hybrid setup, your "presence" isn't about being physically in the office—it's about how you show up in every interaction. Are you actively contributing in meetings, or are you just that little box that occasionally un-mutes to say, "No updates on my end"? Are you reaching out for input and offering your own perspective, or are you just waiting for tasks to be assigned?

One of the simplest ways to build influence is by asking good questions. When you're in a meeting, don't just nod along; ask something that shows you're engaged and thinking critically. It could be as simple as, "How does this align with our bigger objectives?" or "What challenges do we anticipate with this approach?" It's a subtle way to remind people that you're not just a participant—you're someone who's thinking strategically.

And don't be afraid to suggest a new approach or bring up an idea. Even if it's not perfect, it shows that you're invested in the outcome. The truth is, in a remote or hybrid world, staying silent is the quickest way to become invisible. Your voice is your presence, so use it.

The Long Game of Remote Influence

Building influence remotely isn't a one-and-done deal. It's about consistently showing up, sharing your insights, and finding ways to connect with others, even from afar. It's about creating your own visibility instead of waiting for someone to notice you. And sometimes, it means adapting a little of Chad's strategy—though maybe with a few more details than "We'll figure it out!"

For Chad, remote work meant keeping his face on every virtual call, making jokes in the team chat, and somehow always managing to get into the meetings that mattered. For me, it meant learning to be intentional about every interaction—ensuring that when I did speak, it added value. But, I'll admit, I did start adopting Chad's knack for reaching out, even if my coffee chats included a little less small talk and a little more strategy.

At the end of the day, building influence in a remote world is about taking control of your own narrative. It's about creating the future you want, not just waiting for it to unfold. Whether that means scheduling a virtual coffee chat or speaking up more in meetings, the power is in your hands—even if it's over a keyboard.

The Takeaway

Influence isn't built simply by being the loudest voice in the room or having the most face time with leadership. It's about consistency, building trust, and delivering value over time. Whether you're in-person, remote, or hybrid, the principles remain the same: communicate clearly, maintain visibility, and build genuine relationships.

Influence is about showing up in the right ways, whether that's through proactive communication, sharing valuable insights, or supporting others in their success. In a remote or hybrid world, these traits become even more critical, as they help bridge the gap between physical distance and authentic connection. Remember, it's not about where you are; it's about how you show up.

Action Plan: Building Influence Remotely

Objective: To maintain visibility, foster authentic connections, and establish a strong presence in remote or hybrid work environments.

Framework: Influence in a virtual setting is built through clear communication, consistent engagement, and genuine connections. By focusing on impactful updates, fostering camaraderie, and demonstrating reliability, remote professionals can maintain strong team dynamics and drive success.

1. Keep Work Visible Through Thoughtful Updates

Remote work often makes contributions less apparent. Sharing updates that emphasize the impact of efforts ensures alignment with team objectives and enhances visibility.

Example: Provide concise updates highlighting the significance of completed work in achieving team goals. Focus on results and value added to make contributions clear and impactful.

2. Create Space for Casual Connections

Casual interactions are essential for building camaraderie and maintaining team spirit in virtual settings. Small, friendly exchanges help keep relationships strong and foster teamwork.

Example: Share congratulations on achievements or send a quick message with an interesting article. These actions build rapport and strengthen team relationships beyond formal interactions.

3. Bring Humanity into Interactions (With Boundaries)

Personal touches in conversations create rapport while maintaining professionalism. Brief, lighthearted check-ins before meetings set a positive tone and strengthen connections.

Example: Begin meetings with a short, inclusive discussion about universal topics like weekend plans or hobbies. Avoid divisive or overly personal topics to ensure a welcoming and professional environment.

4. Show Engagement by Asking Questions and Sharing Ideas

Active participation during virtual meetings demonstrates commitment and thought leadership. Asking questions and sharing ideas signals engagement and fosters collaboration.

Example: Contribute to discussions by asking relevant questions, such as how a project aligns with team goals, or propose innovative approaches. These actions showcase investment in outcomes and support team success.

5. Build Influence by Showing Up Consistently

Reliability in remote work is built through regular, steady contributions. Consistency in updates, collaboration, and support helps build trust and influence over time.

Example: Maintain dependable engagement through regular updates, encouragement, and participation. Consistent actions reinforce trust and create a foundation for long-term influence within the team.

Reflection and Self-Monitoring

Weekly Reflection: "Did I take specific actions this week to maintain visibility and build connections in my remote work environment?"

Monthly Reflection: "How effectively have I balanced clear communication, consistent engagement, and relationship-building to strengthen my influence in a remote setting?"

Section 4

Adapting to Change and Embracing Fear

Chapter 17

Fear and Freedom – Embracing Failure and Financial Security

If there's one thing that keeps people stuck, it's fear—fear of failure, fear of embarrassment, fear of not living up to expectations. It's that nagging little voice that whispers, *"What if you mess up? What if everyone finds out you don't belong here?"* Fear is like that annoying alarm clock you set 10 minutes too early; you try to ignore it, but it just keeps buzzing until you address it.

For years, I was terrified of making mistakes. I thought every misstep would bring my career to a grinding halt. I was the person who triple-checked every email before hitting send, who hesitated to ask questions in meetings because I didn't want to look uninformed. And let's be real, that fear never truly goes away—it just finds new ways to mess with you. But over time, I've learned that you can't let fear call the shots. In fact, the only way to move forward is to get comfortable with failure.

Failing Fast, Failing Forward

One of the best lessons I learned was from a mentor who told me, "Fail fast, fail forward." The idea is simple: if you're going to mess up, do it quickly, learn from it, and move on. It's not about being reckless; it's about recognizing that mistakes are part of the process.

I remember the first time I applied this mindset. I was working on a new project with a tight deadline, and there was a lot I didn't know. Normally, I would have spent days trying to figure everything out before daring to ask for help. But this time, I tried a different approach. I asked questions early on, even if they seemed basic. I felt a knot in my stomach as I raised my hand during the meeting, but the relief that followed was worth it. And guess what? It saved me—and the team—hours of potential rework. We were able to pivot quickly because we caught the mistakes early.

Meanwhile, Chad, in his typical fashion, took a different approach. He kept his head down, determined to prove he could figure everything out on his own. I watched as he poured hours into the project, rarely stopping to consult anyone. By the time he realized he was heading in the wrong direction, it was too late to course-correct. As much as I admired Chad's determination, it was a classic case of how fear of looking uninformed can backfire.

The Power of Asking Questions

Here's the thing: asking questions doesn't make you look weak; it makes you look smart. It shows that you're willing to learn, that you care about getting it right, and that you're not afraid to acknowledge when you need more information. I used to think that asking questions meant admitting I didn't know something. Now I see it as a way to ensure I get it right the first time—or at least, sooner rather than later.

If you think about it, wouldn't you rather face a little embarrassment now than a massive project failure later? It's a trade-off that pays dividends. The quicker you acknowledge gaps in your knowledge, the quicker you can fill them. The fear of asking questions often stems from a fear of judgment, but in reality, no one expects you to have all the answers—especially when you're in new territory.

It's not just about asking questions in the moment, either. Sometimes, it's about seeking feedback early in the process. Maybe you're working on a new presentation or trying out a new approach to solving a problem. Instead of waiting until you think it's perfect, show it to a trusted colleague or mentor and ask for input. I remember nervously sharing a draft with a colleague, expecting criticism, but instead receiving valuable insights that improved my work. It's a simple way to catch mistakes early and refine your approach without the stress of a last-minute overhaul. And it turns out, people appreciate being asked for their input—it shows that you value their expertise.

Financial Freedom: The Fear Killer

But there's another side to this fear thing that doesn't get talked about enough—financial freedom. When you're living paycheck to paycheck, every career decision feels like a high-stakes gamble. Should I speak up in that meeting? Should I take on that risky project? The fear of losing your job (and with it, your ability to pay the bills) can keep you stuck, playing it safe, and saying yes to things you should say no to.

When you have a financial cushion, though, you get a little bolder. It's not that you stop caring about your job, but you stop feeling like every mistake could spell disaster. Financial freedom gives you a buffer, a little room to breathe, and the ability to take risks without the constant worry of "What if this all falls apart?"

For me, this realization was a game-changer. There was a time when I felt like I was walking on eggshells at work. I was so worried about messing up and losing my job that I found myself nodding along to every request, taking on every extra project, and staying silent when I should have spoken up. I was burning out, and I knew it. I felt trapped, like I was trading my well-being for financial security. But I thought that if I didn't keep pushing, I might lose the paycheck that kept my life running smoothly.

Then I read *The Simple Path to Wealth* by JL Collins, and it flipped my mindset. Collins talks about the importance of saving and investing—building what he calls "F-You Money." It's the kind of money that gives you the freedom to walk away from a job if it's no longer serving you, to speak up when something feels off, and to take risks without constantly second-guessing yourself. You don't need millions in the bank to start feeling that freedom. Even a few months' worth of expenses saved up can make a world of difference.

How Financial Freedom Changes the Game

Here's a practical example: a very successful friend of mine was once offered an intriguing project in a niche area that was a little outside his comfort zone at a startup firm. It was high visibility, but with high visibility came the risk of high failure. When he called to tell me about the offer, I could hear the excitement in his voice mixed with a hint of fear. But this time, that fear didn't paralyze him; it motivated him. The old him would've turned it down, afraid that if he messed it up, it would set his career back. But by then, he had built up an emergency fund and had done well investing. He knew that even if this project didn't go well, he'd be okay. So, he took the leap—and it paid off when the company eventually went public.

I'm not saying that you can't be a risk-taker without financial freedom, but knowing you'll have a roof over your head and a hot meal gives you the peace of mind to make bold decisions without the constant fear of losing everything. Financial freedom can reduce the pressure to play it safe and allow you to take calculated risks, explore new opportunities, and focus on long-term growth.

It's not about being reckless. It's about knowing that even if you fall, you have a safety net. Financial freedom gives you the confidence to take on those bigger challenges, to advocate for yourself in salary negotiations, and to set boundaries when the work becomes too much. It allows you to focus on the bigger picture rather than being bogged down by immediate financial concerns.

Ignorance Is Bliss: Chad's Take

Then there's Chad. Chad seemed blissfully unbothered by fear—not because he had some profound wisdom about embracing failure, but because, well, he barely knew what he was talking about half the time. It was almost like Chad's ignorance gave him an armor of confidence. While the rest of us hesitated, worried about all the things that could go wrong, Chad charged ahead with a big smile and no second thoughts.

He'd take on new projects without overanalyzing the risks, throwing around phrases like "We'll figure it out as we go!" while the rest of us stressed about every possible scenario. Watching Chad, I sometimes envied his carefree approach, even if it was reckless. The funny thing? Sometimes it worked. Chad's sheer confidence (or, let's be honest, cluelessness) meant he wasn't paralyzed by fear the way the rest of us could be. He didn't waste time worrying about what might happen if things went sideways because he genuinely didn't seem to think that far ahead.

Now, I wouldn't recommend Chad's approach as a long-term strategy—after all, when things did go wrong, he usually had no backup plan. But there's something to be said for the kind of courage that comes from not overthinking everything. Chad's confidence, though occasionally misguided, reminded me that sometimes, overanalyzing can hold you back just as much as ignorance can.

Combining Courage and Security

None of this means that fear disappears entirely. It doesn't. Fear is like that unwanted guest at the party—it always finds a way in. But the trick is learning to live with it, to take action even when fear is whispering in your ear. Instead of letting fear hold you back, let it be the thing that pushes you forward.

Financial freedom isn't about becoming invincible; it's about shifting the power dynamic between you and your fears. When you've got a financial safety net, you can make career choices based on what's best for you—not just what pays the bills. And when you combine that with a willingness to embrace failure, to ask questions, and to put yourself out there, you become unstoppable.

The best part? Financial freedom doesn't just give you peace of mind—it gives you negotiating power. It allows you to walk into a salary discussion or promotion conversation knowing that you don't have to accept less than you're worth. You're not just working to survive; you're working to thrive.

So, if you're feeling stuck, ask yourself: How would you approach your career differently if you had a little more financial freedom? What risks would you take? What opportunities would you pursue? And then, start taking those steps—however small—to build your safety net. It might just change everything.

The Takeaway

Fear is a natural part of taking risks, but it's also the gateway to growth. The key is learning to embrace failure as part of the process rather than something to avoid at all costs. By failing fast and asking questions early, you position yourself to learn and course-correct, which ultimately leads to success. Overcoming the fear of failure is about building confidence in your ability to handle setbacks and viewing them as opportunities for growth.

Financial freedom adds another layer of security, allowing you to take more calculated risks without the constant worry of losing everything. When financial security is in place, you gain the freedom to make career decisions that align with your long-term goals and values rather than just immediate financial needs. This balance of courage and freedom empowers you to pursue success on your own terms.

Action Plan: Embracing Failure and Building Financial Freedom

Objective: To leverage failure as a growth tool, make informed decisions, and establish financial independence to support calculated risks.

Framework: Failure is an integral part of success, offering lessons that drive resilience and growth. Coupled with financial freedom, it becomes easier to navigate risks and align career decisions with long-term goals rather than short-term constraints.

1. Adopt the 'Fail Fast, Fail Forward' Mindset

Mistakes provide valuable learning opportunities and reduce the pressure of perfectionism. Addressing challenges early and iterating leads to faster growth and improved results.

Example: Take calculated risks by seeking feedback early in a project and refining efforts as needed. View setbacks as stepping stones for improvement, helping build adaptability and resilience.

2. Ask Questions Without Fear of Judgment

Proactively seeking clarity improves outcomes and prevents unnecessary errors. A culture of inquiry demonstrates commitment and enhances understanding of objectives.

Example: List key questions when beginning a new task or project to ensure alignment. Address these questions early to build confidence and reduce uncertainty while fostering better communication.

3. Take Steps Toward Financial Freedom

Financial independence reduces stress and enables career decisions driven by goals rather than immediate financial needs.

Example: Begin building an emergency fund to cover three to six months of expenses. Use resources like *The Simple Path to Wealth* by JL Collins for actionable advice on achieving financial security and independence.

4. Reframe Failure as a Path to Growth

Failures provide critical insights that inform better decisions and foster resilience over time. Treating setbacks as opportunities encourages continuous development.

Example: After encountering a setback, identify actionable lessons and document them for future reference. Recognizing these insights reinforces the idea that failure is a necessary step in achieving success.

5. Balance Courage with Security for Long-Term Success

Combining a willingness to take risks with financial stability provides a foundation for meaningful progress and informed career choices.

Example: Use a financial safety net to pursue ambitious projects and challenges that align with long-term aspirations. This balance reduces fear of failure while enabling bold, impactful decisions.

Reflection and Self-Monitoring

Weekly Reflection: "What lessons did I take from this week's setbacks, and how can I use them to improve moving forward?"

Monthly Reflection: "Have I made progress toward building financial freedom, and how has it influenced my ability to take risks and embrace growth opportunities?"

Chapter 18

Managing Burnout and Knowing When to Step Back

Burnout is one of those things that sneaks up on you. One moment, you're powering through your to-do list like a productivity machine, and the next, you're staring at your screen, unable to form a coherent thought, wondering why you can't seem to get excited about your work anymore. It feels like you're running on empty, even though the tank was full just yesterday. It's like someone flipped a switch, and suddenly, your brain has decided to go on strike.

I came from a work culture where burnout was seen as a lack of commitment. The unspoken rule was that if you weren't willing to push yourself to the brink, you weren't trying hard enough. I remember colleagues bragging about pulling all-nighters, wearing exhaustion like a badge of honor. But here's the hard truth I learned: you can't outrun burnout. The longer you try to push through it, the more it drags you down. It's like running on a treadmill that's slowly speeding up—eventually, you're going to trip.

Recognizing the Signs Before It's Too Late

The first step in managing burnout is recognizing that it's happening. For me, it was a series of small warning signs—losing interest in projects I used to enjoy, dreading every new email notification, and feeling completely exhausted even after a full night's sleep. And yet, I kept telling myself, "It's just a rough patch. It'll get better." I was convinced that if I just pushed a little harder, I'd break through the fog.

Spoiler alert: It didn't.

Looking back, I should have seen the signs earlier. I'd start my days with a sense of dread, counting down the hours until I could close my laptop. Meetings that I used to enjoy became a chore. I even caught myself envying the barista at the coffee shop, thinking how peaceful their job seemed compared to mine. And let's not forget the telltale symptom of burnout: fantasizing about throwing your laptop out the window and starting a new life as a goat farmer in the mountains. (Okay, maybe that one's just me.)

But seriously, if you find yourself constantly drained, irritable, or feeling like you're just going through the motions, it's time to take a step back. Burnout isn't about being weak—it's about reaching a point where your mind and body are saying, "Enough is enough."

The Hidden Costs of Burnout

Burnout doesn't just impact your performance at work; it takes a toll on your body and mind. The mental health consequences are well-documented—chronic stress is linked to anxiety, depression, and memory problems. It can feel like you're carrying a weight that never gets lighter, and that stress can steal years from your life. And the physical effects aren't any better. Burnout has been associated with higher risks of heart disease, weakened immune function, and even digestive issues. You might find yourself getting sick more often or feeling constantly tired, no matter how much you rest.

Then there's the impact on your personal life. When you're running on empty, it's not just your work that suffers—your relationships do too. You come home with nothing left to give, snapping at your family or retreating into yourself because you're too exhausted to engage. I've seen this firsthand with colleagues who, in their quest to do everything at work, ended up missing out on the lives of the people who mattered most to them. And let's be real—no project is worth the price of your health or the happiness of those around you.

Chad's Strategy: The Master of Boundaries

Of course, Chad had a different approach to avoiding burnout. While the rest of us were burning the midnight oil, Chad had this miraculous ability to sign off at 5:01 PM with a smile on his face. At first, I thought he just didn't care enough, but then I realized something: Chad knew how to set boundaries.

One time, during a particularly grueling project, I found myself on a call at 10 PM, frantically trying to resolve a last-minute issue. Meanwhile, Chad had signed off hours earlier with a simple, "Let's tackle this in the morning." And you know what? He was right. The issue could have waited until the next day, but I didn't give myself that grace. I thought working harder meant caring more, but it just meant running myself into the ground.

Chad understood that productivity isn't about working non-stop—it's about knowing when to step back so that when you do work, you're actually effective. It was a lesson I wish I'd learned sooner, but eventually, I realized that sometimes, the best thing you can do for your career is to close the laptop and recharge.

Prioritization: The Key to Avoiding Overwhelm

It's easy to think that burnout is purely a result of working too many hours, but often, it's about working on the wrong things. If you've read the earlier chapters on prioritization and communication, you'll remember the importance of understanding what truly matters and focusing on those tasks. When everything feels like a priority, nothing actually is. That's why creating a clear list of priorities is essential—especially when you're feeling overwhelmed.

But prioritization isn't just about knowing what tasks to focus on; it's about communicating those priorities to others. As we discussed in Chapter 2: Prioritizing in a World of Chaos, it's crucial to sit down with your stakeholders and agree on what's most important right now. This simple act can save you from wasting time and energy on tasks that aren't truly critical.

I learned this the hard way when I found myself trying to juggle three different projects, thinking that I had to give each of them my all at the same time. I felt guilty about pushing back on any request, even when I knew it would stretch me too thin. But once I started having open conversations with my managers about what was realistic, I found that most of the time, they were more than willing to adjust their expectations. They just needed me to be honest about what I could and couldn't do. It turns out, people aren't mind readers—who knew?

The Art of Delegation: Letting Go Without Losing Control

For many of us, the idea of delegation feels like a double-edged sword. You want to share the workload, but there's that nagging fear: "What if they don't do it as well as I would?" So, instead, you do it all yourself, and you burn out in the process.

Here's the reality: delegation isn't about handing off tasks and forgetting about them—it's about empowering others while freeing up your own time to focus on what only you can do. Yes, the person you delegate to might not do the task exactly the way you would, but that's okay. Sometimes, they bring a fresh perspective that can improve the outcome.

I remember working on a high-stakes presentation for a client. I hesitated to delegate any part of it, thinking it had to be perfect. But when the deadlines started piling up, I realized I had no choice. So, I asked a junior team member to draft the initial slides while I focused on the strategic content.

To my surprise, the slides were great. Sure, they needed a few tweaks, but it saved me hours of time that I could use to polish the overall message. It turned out that my fear of letting go was holding me back from seeing how capable my team really was.

The same applies to anyone in a leadership role—or aspiring to be in one. Being afraid to delegate often comes from a fear of losing control, but the truth is, effective delegation is a sign of trust. It's a way of saying, "I believe you can do this," which in turn helps your team grow and develop their own skills. It also ties back to what we talked about in the earlier chapters on building a strong downward network—when you help lift others up, you build a support system that you can lean on when you need it most.

Shyam Uthaman

Take Your PTO: No, Seriously

Now, here's a controversial take: a high amount of PTO balance is nothing to brag about. Your company promises to pay you to have days off to recover—take them! I get it, some of us pride ourselves on our dedication and being there whenever needed, but burnout doesn't care about your pride. Taking your PTO isn't a sign of weakness; it's a smart move to maintain your sanity.

You don't need to jet off to a tropical island (though I wouldn't object). Use the time to do absolutely anything outside of work. I personally recommend watching *Cobra Kai* if you're a *Karate Kid* fan, but I'm sure you have something in your life that brings you joy—riding a bike, taking a swim, or maybe even calling up Chad. I'm sure he'll be happy to catch up for a quick drink. Whatever you do, the point is to step away, recharge, and come back with a fresh perspective.

Taking time off isn't just about resting your mind—it's about giving yourself the space to remember what life looks like outside of work. And when you do that, you often come back with renewed energy and new ideas. So, the next time you're tempted to skip that vacation day, remember: it's there for a reason.

Finding Balance: It's Okay to Rest

Burnout can make you feel like you're failing, like you're not cut out for the demands of your job. But the truth is, knowing when to rest is one of the most important skills you can develop. It's about playing the long game—making sure you have the energy, focus, and creativity to keep going, not just this week, but for years to come.

So if you're feeling burnt out, if the thought of another email makes you want to throw your phone out the window, take a step back. Give yourself permission to rest. It's not about being weak; it's about being smart. Because sometimes, the most productive thing you can do is nothing at all.

The Takeaway

Burnout isn't a badge of honor; it's a signal that something needs to change. Recognizing the signs early and taking proactive steps to manage your workload, set boundaries, and prioritize self-care are essential for long-term success and well-being. Delegation and taking time off aren't signs of weakness—they're strategies for sustaining your energy and effectiveness over the long haul. Remember, you can't pour from an empty cup. By taking care of yourself, you ensure that you can continue to contribute at your best.

Action Plan: Managing Burnout and Finding Balance

Objective: To recognize burnout early, establish boundaries, and prioritize health and well-being for long-term success.

Framework: Burnout can derail productivity and personal health if not addressed early. This framework focuses on identifying warning signs, setting boundaries, and fostering habits that maintain balance and well-being while sustaining professional growth.

1. Recognize Early Signs of Burnout

Constant fatigue, irritability, and a lack of motivation are common signs of burnout. Identifying these symptoms early allows for timely intervention and prevents long-term exhaustion.

Example: Regularly track energy levels and mood. When signs of burnout appear, evaluate workloads and implement adjustments such as taking short breaks or pausing for self-reflection to recharge.

2. Prioritize Ruthlessly and Communicate

Overwhelm often stems from unclear priorities and lack of communication. Setting clear priorities and discussing them with managers or teams helps align efforts with key goals while reducing unnecessary stress.

Example: Create a list of top priorities for the week and share it with relevant stakeholders. Proactively set boundaries for lower-priority tasks to maintain focus on impactful work.

3. Delegate Wisely and Trust Your Team

Effective delegation empowers teams and lightens the individual workload. Clear communication and trust in others' abilities ensure that tasks are handled efficiently, often leading to fresh perspectives and enhanced results.

Example: Identify one task to delegate this week. Provide concise instructions and offer autonomy to complete the work. This fosters collaboration and builds trust within the team while reducing personal strain.

4. Make Taking PTO a Non-Negotiable

Time off is essential for recharging and maintaining long-term productivity. Scheduling regular breaks provides mental and physical recovery, ultimately boosting creativity and focus.

Example: Plan and take PTO consistently, even for a long weekend. Use this time to disconnect from work, engage in relaxing or enjoyable activities, and return with renewed energy.

5. Never Sacrifice Health or Family for Work

Burnout often harms relationships and well-being. Prioritizing personal health and time with loved ones fosters balance and helps maintain perspective, ensuring sustainable career success.

Example: Establish firm boundaries to protect health and family time. Learn to decline tasks or projects that encroach on these priorities. Remember, professional roles can be replaced, but health and relationships cannot.

Reflection and Self-Monitoring

Weekly Reflection: "Did I recognize and address any signs of burnout this week? What steps helped me maintain balance?"

Monthly Reflection: "How effectively have I managed my workload and boundaries to prioritize health and well-being? What improvements can I make to sustain balance?"

Chapter 19

Handling the Unexpected—The Curveballs of Corporate Life

Change is the only constant in corporate life. You can plan every detail, align your team, and map out your goals, but eventually, the universe throws a curveball your way. It's just the way things go. The question isn't if things will go off course—it's when. And more importantly, how you'll handle it when they do.

I used to think that the best way to manage change was to control everything. I'd create meticulous project plans, detailing every step down to the last comma. But as I learned (through more than a few painful experiences), the best-laid plans often meet reality—and reality usually wins.

Shyam Uthaman

Planning for Change, Not Perfection

One of the biggest lessons I've learned is that a plan isn't about predicting the future; it's about preparing for the inevitable changes that will come. Early in my career, I thought a good plan was one that never changed. Now, I know a good plan is one that can adapt.

For instance, I once led a project where the scope seemed straightforward—until halfway through when the client came back with a massive change request. Suddenly, the entire timeline was out the window, and I found myself staring at a project plan that felt more like fiction than reality.

In moments like these, it's tempting to panic, scramble, or even try to push back the change altogether. But here's the truth: change isn't the problem. The problem is not communicating what that change means for your project.

Adjusting the Plan: The Importance of Communication

When change hits, your first step isn't to figure out how to make it work—it's to communicate. I've learned that adjusting the scope of a project means recalibrating expectations with all the stakeholders involved. This means reaching out to your team, leadership, and anyone else impacted, and laying out what the change means for the timeline, budget, and deliverables.

This ties back to what we discussed in Communication and Transparency—Speak Now or Forever Hold Your Stress. It's not just about raising the flag; it's about clearly explaining how a change impacts the original plan. That means defining what's changed, what's at risk, and what needs to be adjusted. It's a delicate balance between being realistic and maintaining a "we'll find a way" attitude.

In my case, I sat down with the client and said, "Here's what we originally agreed to, here's the new request, and here's what that means for our current plan. We have a few options—either we adjust the timeline to accommodate this change, or we can prioritize the most critical parts and push some features to a later release." It wasn't the most comfortable conversation, but it allowed us to work together on a solution instead of letting things fall apart later.

When Deadlines Don't Budge: Finding a Way Forward

But what happens when you don't have the luxury of adjusting the timeline? What if the change comes in, but the deadline remains set in stone? This is where it's crucial to discuss trade-offs.

I've found that when timelines can't shift, the best question to ask is, "What do we prioritize?" This might mean delivering the most critical features first while pushing non-essential items to a later date. Or, if every piece of work is truly a must-have, you'll need to be upfront about what it will take to get everything done on time.

Will you need more budget for overtime hours or new hires? Do you need to shift other projects around to free up resources?

A colleague of mine once said, "There's no such thing as a miracle worker in project management—just someone who knows which lever to pull when things change." If you can't adjust the scope, adjust the resources. If you can't change the resources, adjust the expectations.

One time, we had a major software launch, and just weeks before the deadline, the compliance team identified new regulations we needed to meet. We couldn't change the launch date—it had been announced publicly. So, we sat down with leadership and explained, "Here's what it will take to meet this new requirement within the deadline. We can either allocate more budget for temporary contractors, or we can shift resources from other projects temporarily." It wasn't an easy ask, but at least it allowed them to make an informed decision, and we managed to deliver—barely.

The key here isn't to avoid change, but to guide your stakeholders through it. When you clearly lay out the options, you're not just managing change—you're leading through it.

Chad's Strategy: Ignorance Was Bliss

Meanwhile, Chad had his own way of dealing with change—he just... didn't. I remember a time when a major technical issue popped up during one of his projects. Everyone was scrambling, but Chad kept his usual calm, unbothered demeanor. At first, I thought he was playing it cool—maybe he knew something we didn't. But when I finally asked him how he was handling it, he just shrugged and said, "I'm sure it'll work out."

And you know what? For Chad, it often did. He'd coast along, confident that things would sort themselves out. Sometimes, that laid-back approach worked. But when things didn't go as planned, it fell on the rest of the team to pick up the pieces.

It was a reminder that while optimism is a great quality, it's not a substitute for action. Chad's "ignorance is bliss" strategy wasn't something I could afford to rely on, but it did teach me that there's value in staying calm when things go south—so long as you're following it up with a solid plan.

Managing Team Frustration and Conflict

Change doesn't just affect timelines and deliverables; it affects people. When a project shifts direction or new demands are suddenly added, your team can feel the pressure—and that pressure can turn into frustration or conflict. Managing these emotions is just as important as managing the logistics of the change itself.

I remember leading a project where a big client change request came in right after we thought we'd wrapped up the development phase. The team had already put in extra hours, and the idea of going back and reworking features was met with a collective groan.

It wasn't just about the extra effort—it was about feeling like all their hard work was being undone.

Instead of pushing forward blindly, I took a step back and gathered the team for a conversation. I acknowledged their frustration, shared my own, and made it clear that I understood how much the new request added to their plates. Then I said, "Let's talk about what's possible. We can't change the situation, but maybe we can change how we handle it."

I asked for their input on which parts of the project we could prioritize and if there were ways we could streamline the rework. By giving them a voice in the process, it became less about "another demand from above" and more about solving the problem together.

Was it easy? Not at all. But it turned a tense situation into a productive one. And when we finally delivered the project, the team felt a sense of pride—not just in the outcome, but in how they managed to adapt together.

Anticipating Change: A Skill Worth Developing

Over time, I've realized that the ability to anticipate change is one of the most valuable skills you can develop. This doesn't mean you need a crystal ball—it means you learn to read the signs. Maybe it's a client asking for more frequent updates than usual, or a teammate mentioning they're feeling overwhelmed. Often, these small signals are early indicators that something is about to shift.

I've made it a habit to build a little extra time into my project timelines for the "unknown unknowns." It's not always possible, but when you can plan for a buffer, it makes a world of difference when something unexpected comes your way. It's like wearing a raincoat on a cloudy day—you might not need it, but you'll be glad you have it if the skies open up.

Embracing Change with Confidence

In the end, handling the unexpected isn't about being perfect—it's about being flexible. It's about having the confidence to adapt, the communication skills to guide your team through the shift, and the foresight to see challenges as opportunities for growth.

Remember, the unexpected will come. It's how you react that defines your success. So, when the curveballs come your way—and they will—don't panic. Take a deep breath, assess the situation, communicate the impact, and adjust your plan. And maybe, just maybe, find a moment to laugh at the chaos along the way.

The Takeaway

In the ever-evolving world of work, curveballs are inevitable. The key to thriving amidst change is adaptability and communication. It's not enough to have a plan—you need to be flexible enough to adjust that plan when circumstances change. Communicating those changes effectively with your team and stakeholders ensures that everyone is on the same page, even when the path ahead shifts.

Managing unexpected changes is less about having all the answers upfront and more about staying calm, gathering information, and making informed decisions. Lean on your team, ask for support, and ensure that you communicate both the risks and potential solutions to leadership. When change happens, it's an opportunity to demonstrate your resilience and problem-solving skills.

Action Plan: Navigating the Unexpected and Leading Through Change

Objective: To stay adaptable, communicate effectively, and lead confidently when faced with unexpected challenges.

Framework: Change is inevitable, but it doesn't have to derail progress. By approaching challenges with flexibility, clear communication, and collaboration, you can turn disruptions into opportunities for growth. This framework emphasizes prioritization, team engagement, and preparedness to navigate uncertainty effectively.

1. Prepare for Flexibility, Not Perfection

Treating plans as adaptable frameworks rather than immovable objects helps manage changes without losing momentum. A focus on core objectives ensures progress even when circumstances shift.

Example: Begin projects with a flexible mindset. Prioritize critical deliverables but remain open to revising approaches when challenges arise. This adaptability turns obstacles into growth opportunities.

2. Communicate Adjustments Clearly and Early

Clear and early communication with stakeholders prevents confusion and sets the stage for collaboration when plans change. Transparency about the impact of adjustments fosters trust and alignment.

Example: Notify stakeholders promptly about changes, explaining their rationale and anticipated outcomes. This approach ensures clarity and reduces stress across the team.

3. Reassess and Prioritize When Plans Shift

Unexpected changes often require a reevaluation of priorities. Identifying high-impact tasks and deferring less critical items ensures resources are directed effectively, maintaining progress without overburdening the team.

Example: Collaborate with stakeholders to focus on tasks that drive the most value. Prioritize effectively to ensure key objectives are met even in the face of shifting circumstances.

4. Engage Your Team to Co-Create Solutions

Involving the team in addressing challenges fosters innovative solutions and builds commitment to revised plans. Team input often brings fresh perspectives and enhances collaboration.

Example: Solicit team ideas during unexpected changes. Validate their concerns and work together to create a plan that balances priorities and maintains motivation.

5. Account for Buffer Time to Underpromise and Overdeliver

Building buffer time into project plans creates a safety net for unforeseen challenges. This practice reduces last-minute stress and allows for consistent delivery of quality results.

Example: Incorporate realistic buffer time into project timelines to manage unforeseen changes. This ensures preparedness while creating opportunities to exceed expectations when everything proceeds smoothly.

Reflection and Self-Monitoring

Weekly Reflection: "How did I adapt to unexpected changes this week, and what strategies helped maintain progress?"

Monthly Reflection: "How effectively did I communicate and prioritize during periods of uncertainty? What can I improve to navigate future challenges more confidently?"

Chapter 20

Trusting Your Instincts—Knowing When to Go With Your Gut

In the corporate world, we're often told to trust the data, follow the process, and make decisions based on logic and analysis. And that's good advice—most of the time. But what about those moments when the data is murky, the analysis is unclear, and all you're left with is that nagging feeling that something's off? That's when your gut—yes, that instinctive, hard-to-explain feeling—comes into play.

I used to think that gut instincts were a little overrated, something for motivational speeches rather than boardrooms. But over time, I've learned that sometimes, your instincts know more than your spreadsheet does. The funny thing about your gut is that it's not some mystical sixth sense—it's the sum of all your experiences, quietly whispering in your ear.

When Experience Speaks

"Training teaches you what to do, but experience teaches you what not to." It's a simple truth that's hard-earned. Training programs, webinars, and those endless "best practice" guides all have their place. They tell you how things should work, in a perfect world with no surprises. But experience? Experience is what kicks in when you're in the middle of a project, and the wheels are coming off despite following every guideline to the letter.

Your gut is like a distillation of everything you've learned over the years—every mistake, every win, every time you thought, "I should have seen that coming." It's the voice that says, "Hey, remember the last time a project seemed too good to be true? Maybe you should double-check this one."

Balancing Instinct with Data

Trusting your gut doesn't mean abandoning logic or ignoring the facts. It's about using your instincts as a guide and then validating them with data. Think of your gut as that friend who always warns you about potential pitfalls. They might not have all the details, but they've been around the block enough to know when something doesn't smell right.

It's like having a smoke alarm in your house. When it goes off, you don't just assume the house is on fire—you check for smoke. Maybe it's a false alarm, or maybe there's something smoldering that you need to address. Your instincts work the same way. When you feel that pang of uncertainty, it's time to pause, dig a little deeper, and see if there's a fire or just burnt toast.

An Email That Didn't Feel Right

Let me give you a real-world example: my boss once asked me to send an email to a client that just didn't sit right with me. It was one of those emails that seemed simple enough, but the tone and the content felt... off. My boss was convinced that it was the right message, but my gut told me otherwise.

Now, I'm not one to defy instructions lightly, but that nagging feeling wouldn't go away. So, instead of sending it as-is, I took the time to ask my boss a few clarifying questions. "What's our goal with this email?" and "How do you think the client might interpret this?" After some discussion, it became clear that the email might have come across as defensive, and we revised it into something more collaborative.

Was my boss thrilled with the pushback? Not at first. But when the client responded positively to the revised message, I could see my boss silently appreciating that I'd followed my gut.

Chad's Gut Gamble—The Vendor Swap That Didn't Land

Then there's Chad. Now, Chad had a tendency to rely on his gut feeling a little too much—especially when it came to making big decisions. Take, for instance, the time he decided that our vendor wasn't cutting it halfway through a critical project. Chad was convinced that the vendor wouldn't be able to meet the deadlines, despite there being no major red flags yet. He felt like their energy was off, like they were about to drop the ball.

So, in typical Chad fashion, he called for a meeting with senior leadership and pushed to change vendors, armed with nothing more than his gut feeling and a couple of vague complaints. He was confident—maybe a bit too confident. But when leadership asked for data points to support his claim—missed milestones, quality issues, or even customer complaints—Chad came up empty.

Without hard evidence, Chad's credibility took a hit. Leadership dismissed his concerns, and we continued with the original vendor. Ironically, the vendor ended up delivering just fine, and Chad's unfounded alarm only served to make him look like he'd jumped the gun.

The lesson? Trusting your gut is important, but so is backing it up with facts. If Chad had done a bit more digging—gathered some metrics, observed performance trends—he might have made a stronger case. But when you're in the business world, you can't just rely on your gut alone; you need to show your homework.

When to Go With Your Gut—And When to Ignore It

So, how do you know when to trust your gut and when to stick with the facts? Here's what I've learned:

- **When You've Seen It Before:** If your instinct is based on patterns you've seen over the years, listen to it. Experience gives your gut a memory of sorts. If you've encountered similar situations in the past, that instinctive nudge might be drawing on knowledge you didn't even realize you had.

- **When the Data Confirms It:** The best-case scenario is when your gut and the data align. If you feel like a project is risky and the analysis shows a high number of uncertainties, it's probably worth taking that feeling seriously.

- **When It Just Won't Go Away:** If a gut feeling persists, even after you've looked at the data and talked to the experts, pay attention to it. That nagging doubt can be a signal that you're missing something important. Use it as a prompt to dig deeper, even if it means taking another look at the problem with fresh eyes.

On the other hand, if your gut is telling you something that you know contradicts the evidence, it's time to take a step back. I've had moments where my gut said, "This will never work," but the numbers—and the experts—said otherwise. That's when I know it's time to focus on the facts and put my feelings aside.

Embrace the Balance

At the end of the day, the best decisions are made by balancing instinct and information. It's about being willing to question your own assumptions and staying open to those unexplainable feelings that nudge you in one direction or another. Sometimes, the right answer isn't in the numbers—it's in your ability to see the bigger picture.

So, next time you have that nagging feeling that something's not quite right, don't ignore it. Take a step back, ask a few questions, and see where it leads. And if you ever find yourself following your gut down a winding path, just remember: sometimes, that path leads to solutions you wouldn't have found otherwise. And if it doesn't? Well, at least you'll have an interesting story to tell.

The Takeaway

Trusting your instincts is not about disregarding data, but about understanding the nuances that data alone may not reveal. Experience sharpens your instincts, allowing you to see patterns where others see noise. It's the internal compass that guides you when there's no clear path, built from years of trial and error, successes and failures.

However, instincts must be tempered with humility. Trusting your gut doesn't mean ignoring facts; it means understanding when to pause and recalibrate. In moments of doubt, balance intuition with logic. A decision made purely on instinct can be powerful—but only when it's informed by experience and grounded in reality.

Action Plan: Balancing Instinct and Analysis

Objective: To leverage gut instincts effectively without undermining logical decision-making, allowing you to combine intuition with analysis for smarter, more confident decisions.

Framework: Instincts are shaped by experience and observation, acting as an early warning system for potential challenges. This framework helps validate and harness gut feelings without letting them override facts. By reflecting on past experiences, seeking input from trusted colleagues, and balancing instincts with data, you can make decisions that are both intuitive and informed.

1. Identify the Source of Your Gut Feeling

Gut feelings often stem from past experiences, even if they're not immediately obvious. Recognizing patterns or similarities in situations can provide valuable insights that might not be apparent at first glance.

Example: Reflect on similar situations encountered in the past. Consider whether the feeling stems from prior observations or outcomes, and identify any clear indicators that support the instinct.

2. Validate Instincts with Small Tests

Instead of committing fully to a decision based solely on instinct, starting small and gathering feedback can minimize risks. Small actions can confirm or refine the initial gut feeling without significant consequences.

Example: Implement a pilot project or take a limited action based on instinct. This approach allows validation or adjustment while maintaining flexibility until more information becomes available.

3. Consider Alternative Perspectives Before Deciding

Discussing instincts with trusted colleagues often helps clarify thoughts and reveal new angles. Seeking input from others provides additional context and can strengthen the basis for a decision.

Example: Consult with a trusted colleague or peer who has tackled similar challenges. Their perspective may either reinforce or challenge the instinct, providing a more rounded view of the situation.

4. Use Your Instinct as a Prompt, Not Proof

Gut feelings are best used as cues to investigate further rather than as definitive evidence. Treat them as signals to re-evaluate data, question assumptions, or explore additional details before making a decision.

Example: Use instinct as a starting point to revisit project data, check for potential weak points, or confirm expectations with stakeholders. This ensures the decision is both informed and balanced.

5. Keep a Balance: Know When to Let Go of Instinct

When instincts conflict with clear evidence or expert advice, prioritizing logic and facts is essential. Recognizing when instinct may lean toward overcaution can help refine its reliability over time.

Example: If data and analysis contradict gut feelings, rely on the evidence to guide the decision. Track such instances to understand when instincts may need recalibration, improving accuracy and confidence in future decisions.

Reflection and Self-Monitoring:

Weekly Reflection: "Did I use my instincts effectively this week? How did I balance them with data to make informed decisions?"

Monthly Reflection: "What patterns have emerged in how I validate and act on my instincts? How can I refine this balance for better decision-making?"

Section 5

The Long Game and Final Wisdom

Chapter 21

The Power of Asking Why

Asking "why" is one of the simplest and yet most powerful tools you have in your professional arsenal. It can change the direction of a project, alter how you're perceived in your role, and even shape the trajectory of your career. But it's also one of those things that people often shy away from, afraid they'll come across as annoying, insubordinate, or simply clueless.

Early in my career, I, too, was afraid of the question "why." I figured that if someone gave me a directive, my job was to execute it, not challenge it. I mean, what if they thought I was questioning their expertise or doubting their leadership? But as time went on, I realized that the power of "why" wasn't about challenging authority—it was about seeking clarity, aligning on goals, and making sure that I was focusing my efforts on the right things.

Shyam Uthaman

When "Why" Saves the Day

One of the most valuable lessons I learned came during a large-scale project where our team was tasked with a seemingly straightforward objective: roll out a new system upgrade by the end of the quarter. Easy enough, right? We got the ball rolling, broke the work into tasks, and started chipping away at the mountain of work in front of us.

But as I delved deeper into the requirements, that nagging question kept popping into my head: Why are we doing this again? So, I took a deep breath and went to the project sponsor to ask, "Could you clarify what success looks like for this upgrade? Why is this particular deadline so crucial?"

Turns out, the upgrade was tied to a new feature launch that would coincide with a major client event. If we missed that deadline, we'd not only lose the chance to showcase our new feature but also potentially jeopardize our relationship with a key client. Understanding the "why" behind the timeline gave me and my team a whole new sense of urgency—and it helped us prioritize tasks that would directly impact the launch.

Suddenly, it wasn't just about hitting a date on the calendar; it was about aligning our work with a larger business goal. And, most importantly, we knew why it mattered.

The Human-Centric Design Approach: Why "Why" Matters

Asking "why" is a critical aspect of what's called a human-centric design approach. This methodology focuses on designing solutions that meet the actual needs of users by understanding their context, behaviors, and pain points. It's about designing for people, not just for requirements.

Most people, when handed a requirement, jump straight into delivering what's asked of them. But a human-centric approach involves zooming out and understanding what the user is truly trying to achieve. You might be addressing a symptom rather than solving the real problem.

Let me give you an example. I once had a client who asked for a fancy dashboard to display some sales metrics. Most people would take that request, build the dashboard, and call it a day. But I decided to dig deeper. I asked the client what they planned to do with the data in the dashboard. What was the end goal? How did this fit into their daily workflow?

After some probing, I learned that the client's primary need wasn't actually a dashboard at all. They just wanted to pull the data into an Excel file, do some quick calculations, and then send it out in an email to a few people. In other words, all that time I could have spent creating a sleek dashboard would have been wasted because the client wasn't planning to use it.

So, instead of building the dashboard, we set up an automated data feed that sent the relevant numbers directly to their inbox, ready to be shared. It took half the time, required less maintenance, and solved the client's problem more effectively. If we had just stopped at the initial request, we would have built something shiny but ultimately useless.

Human-centric design is all about peeling back the layers of the onion—taking time to understand the real problem before offering a solution. And sometimes, the first "why" leads to another, and then another. But each time, you get closer to the core of what's really needed.

Avoiding the Pitfalls of "Why"

Of course, asking "why" isn't always without its pitfalls. There's a delicate balance between being inquisitive and becoming the office equivalent of a toddler in the "Why Phase."

One of my colleagues once took the "why" thing a bit too far. Every time our boss suggested something, he'd launch into a series of questions that made the rest of us want to crawl under the conference room table. It wasn't that his questions were wrong; they were just… a bit relentless.

"Why are we focusing on this feature?" Okay, fair point. "But why do we even need this client?" All right, maybe don't ask that. "Why do we have to work on Fridays?" And now, we've lost him.

Don't be that guy. Asking "why" is about digging deeper to understand the purpose behind what you're doing, not questioning every minor detail. A well-timed "why" can open up valuable conversations. Too many, though, and you risk being perceived as combative or, even worse, clueless.

The Chad Effect: When You Don't Ask Why

Now, let's talk about Chad—because, really, what would a chapter be without him? Chad wasn't big on asking "why." He had a habit of diving into projects with the kind of enthusiasm that made you wonder if he even knew what the project was about. To Chad, if he had a task, he'd run with it—sometimes quite literally. This time, he was tasked with improving the company's client feedback process.

Chad jumped in, created a new feedback form, and set up a fancy survey tool. He made it look sleek, added a bunch of rating scales, drop-down options, and even a "suggestion box" feature. The survey was long—too long, but Chad thought it was thorough. In his mind, more questions meant more insights.

What he never asked, though, was why the feedback process needed improvement in the first place. Why were clients not responding to the previous surveys? What was the real goal behind gathering feedback? And what would the company actually do with this data once it was collected?

Fast forward a few weeks, and the results started trickling in—or rather, not trickling in. The response rate was dismal. Most clients didn't even finish the survey, and those who did left comments like, "Took too long," "Not sure why I had to rate your hold music," and "Please stop sending these."

Chad's new process had managed to take a simple problem and turn it into a more complex one. What clients really needed was a quick and easy way to give their feedback, not a multi-page survey with questions that required a coffee break midway through. If Chad had spent time asking "why" before diving into the work, he might have realized that a two-question survey or even a simple feedback email could have been far more effective.

And here's the kicker—because Chad didn't understand the bigger picture, he ended up missing out on valuable insights the company did care about, like why clients were dropping off during onboarding. But by then, the clients were so fed up with the lengthy surveys that they stopped responding altogether.

It was a tough lesson for Chad: sometimes, asking "why" isn't just about saving time—it's about building something that people will actually use. If Chad had asked a few key questions up front, he might have built a feedback system that was simple, effective, and aligned with the company's goals. Instead, he was left with a survey that was impressive to look at but gathered more dust than data.

The Right Way to Ask "Why"

So how do you ask "why" without stepping on toes or coming across as a nuisance? Here are a few pointers:

- **Know Your Timing:** Not every meeting or discussion is the right time to bring out the big questions. Pick your moments—maybe during a one-on-one with your boss, a project planning session, or when you're in the early stages of a new initiative.

- **Frame It with Curiosity:** Instead of saying, "Why are we doing this?" try, "Can you help me understand the reason behind this approach?" or "I want to make sure I'm aligned—what's the key goal we're aiming for?" It's amazing how a slight change in wording can shift a question from sounding accusatory to sounding helpful.

- **Focus on the Outcome:** Make it clear that your "why" is about delivering better results, not questioning someone's judgment. For example, "How does this fit into our larger strategy?" or "What's the most important outcome we're looking for here?" shows that you're thinking about the bigger picture.

When "Why" Changes the Game

Sometimes, asking "why" can even change the course of your career. I once had a mentor who told me, "Never just do what's asked of you—find out what's really needed." It stuck with me because it's easy to become a task-doer, someone who simply checks boxes. But those who ask the deeper questions—the ones who seek to understand the real objectives—are the ones who get noticed.

By asking "why," you can identify opportunities that others might miss. You can see when a project is veering off course, or when an idea could be taken a step further. It's a simple question that can lead to a wealth of insights, and ultimately, it can transform how you approach your work.

So, the next time you're faced with a directive that doesn't quite make sense or a project that seems to be lacking direction, don't be afraid to ask why. You might just find that it's the key to unlocking a new perspective—and to making sure that your work doesn't just get done, but actually matters.

The Takeaway

Asking "why" goes beyond curiosity—it's a powerful tool for uncovering the truth. When you ask "why," you're peeling back the layers of complexity to reveal the core issues. It's not about questioning for the sake of questioning, but about challenging assumptions and digging deeper to find meaningful insights.

When you don't ask why, you risk solving the wrong problem. You may create temporary fixes, but the root cause remains. By asking the right questions, you unlock the ability to innovate, improve, and transform processes, ultimately creating more sustainable solutions that benefit everyone involved.

In the end, asking "why" isn't just a strategy—it's a mindset. It's about being willing to challenge the status quo, think critically, and strive for understanding in everything you do. It's this mindset that leads to true leadership and growth.

Action Plan: The Art of Asking "Why" to Drive Purposeful Work

Objective: To use the power of "why" to bring clarity, focus, and meaningful impact to your work, ensuring alignment with goals and creating sustainable solutions.

Framework: The habit of asking "why" encourages curiosity and drives understanding, enabling you to uncover the true purpose behind tasks and initiatives. By framing questions constructively, balancing their frequency, and digging deeper into root causes, you can avoid wasted effort and deliver work that truly matters.

1. Embrace the Habit of Asking "Why" for Clarity

Asking "why" helps to clarify goals and focus efforts on what truly matters. It ensures tasks and projects align with broader objectives, avoiding wasted time on irrelevant or low-impact work.

Example: Before starting a task, ask clarifying questions to understand its purpose and alignment with broader goals, such as, "What is the primary objective here?" or "What impact are we aiming to achieve?"

2. Frame "Why" with Curiosity, Not Challenge

The way "why" is framed can determine its impact. Asking constructively signals curiosity and alignment rather than confrontation or doubt, creating a collaborative environment for deeper insights.

Example: Use questions like, "Can you help me understand the reasoning behind this approach?" instead of directly questioning decisions, to foster productive discussions and demonstrate a willingness to learn.

3. Dig Deeper for a Human-Centric Understanding

Understanding the end-user's needs or the broader context ensures solutions address the real problem rather than just symptoms. This human-centric approach improves outcomes and builds trust.

Example: Instead of delivering a solution at face value, ask follow-up questions like, "How will this be used in practice?" or "What challenges are we solving for the user?" to ensure the work is impactful.

4. Balance Your "Whys" to Avoid Overstepping

Excessive questioning can create friction or undermine credibility. Limiting "why" questions to essential areas ensures they add value without overwhelming team members or stakeholders.

Example: Focus your inquiries on areas with the greatest impact, such as timelines, objectives, and risks, rather than questioning every detail of a plan or project.

5. Use "Why" to Look for Long-Term Solutions

Recurring issues often stem from deeper, unaddressed causes. Asking "why" multiple times uncovers root problems, enabling sustainable solutions that prevent repeated setbacks.

Example: When faced with a recurring delay, ask a series of "why" questions to identify systemic issues, such as communication breakdowns or process inefficiencies, and implement targeted changes to resolve them.

Reflection and Self-Monitoring

Weekly Reflection: "Did I use 'why' effectively this week to clarify goals and ensure alignment? How did it improve the outcomes of my work?"

Monthly Reflection: "How have my 'why' questions uncovered deeper insights or driven long-term solutions? What adjustments can I make to ask 'why' more constructively?"

Chapter 22

Mastering Office Diplomacy

In our earlier discussion on navigating corporate politics, we explored how understanding the dynamics of your workplace can propel you forward without compromising your integrity. Now, let's delve into the other side of that coin—diplomacy. While politics is about understanding the game, diplomacy is about mastering the art of influence without authority. It's the subtle skill of guiding outcomes and building alliances through tact, empathy, and strategic communication.

The Essence of Diplomacy

Diplomacy isn't just for ambassadors and heads of state; it's a crucial skill in any professional setting. At its core, diplomacy is about handling situations and people in a sensitive and effective way. It's knowing how to convey your ideas without causing offense, how to navigate conflicts without burning bridges, and how to persuade others while respecting their perspectives.

Early in my career, I thought being direct and assertive was the best way to get things done. If there was a problem, I addressed it head-on, sometimes without considering how my approach affected others. While this occasionally yielded quick results, it often left a trail of strained relationships and missed opportunities. I soon realized that getting things done isn't just about pushing forward; it's about bringing others along with you.

The Power of Emotional Intelligence

Diplomacy is deeply rooted in emotional intelligence—the ability to understand and manage your own emotions while recognizing and influencing the emotions of others. It's about reading the room, sensing unspoken concerns, and adapting your communication style accordingly.

I recall a project where tensions were high due to looming deadlines and conflicting priorities. One team member, Alex, was particularly resistant to a new process we were implementing. Instead of confronting Alex about the resistance, I took a moment to empathize. I approached them privately and asked for their perspective. It turned out that Alex was worried the new process would make their role redundant. By acknowledging their fears and involving them in refining the process, we not only eased their concerns but also improved the implementation with their valuable input.

This experience taught me that diplomacy often involves looking beyond surface-level conflicts to address underlying emotions and motivations.

Navigating Difficult Conversations

One of the most challenging aspects of professional life is handling difficult conversations—whether it's delivering tough feedback, addressing performance issues, or negotiating conflicting interests. Diplomacy equips you with the tools to navigate these conversations with grace.

A key strategy is to focus on the issue, not the person. Use "I" statements instead of "you" statements to express your perspective without casting blame. For example, saying "I feel that the project's timeline is at risk due to recent delays" is more constructive than "You are delaying the project."

It's also important to listen actively. Allow the other person to share their viewpoint without interruption. This not only shows respect but can also provide insights that help resolve the issue.

Influencing Without Authority

Often in the workplace, you need the cooperation of colleagues who don't report to you. This is where diplomacy shines—it's the art of influencing others without relying on formal authority.

Consider a time when I needed support from the IT department to implement a new software tool for my team. I had no direct authority over the IT staff, and they were already swamped with requests. Instead of demanding assistance, I approached the head of IT with a proposal outlining how the new tool would not only benefit my team but also streamline cross-departmental workflows, ultimately reducing the IT department's workload in the long run.

By aligning my request with their interests and presenting it as a win-win, I secured their support. This approach required patience, empathy, and strategic thinking—all hallmarks of effective diplomacy.

The Role of Patience and Timing

Diplomacy often involves knowing when to act and when to hold back. Patience and timing can be as crucial as the words you choose. Sometimes, pushing for a decision immediately can backfire if the other parties aren't ready.

I once worked with a stakeholder who was notorious for delaying approvals. Instead of bombarding them with reminders—which only seemed to entrench their reluctance—I tried a different tactic. I scheduled a casual meeting to discuss their priorities and challenges. Through this conversation, I learned they were overwhelmed with projects and feared that approving ours would add to their burden.

Armed with this insight, I adjusted our proposal to include additional support for implementation and highlighted how it would ultimately alleviate some of their workload. Shortly after, we received the approval. By exercising patience and choosing the right moment to address their concerns, we achieved our goal without causing friction.

Cultural Sensitivity in a Global Workplace

In today's interconnected world, you may collaborate with colleagues from diverse cultural backgrounds. Diplomacy requires an understanding of cultural nuances and adapting your communication style accordingly.

For example, in some cultures, direct criticism is considered rude, while in others, it's appreciated for its clarity. Being aware of these differences can prevent misunderstandings and foster stronger relationships.

I learned this firsthand when working with an international team. During a conference call, I noticed that some team members were unusually quiet. Initially, I thought they agreed with the plan, but later realized they had reservations they didn't express openly. To address this, I started sending out meeting agendas in advance and followed up with individual messages inviting their input. This approach respected their communication preferences and led to more productive collaborations.

Developing Active Listening Skills

Diplomacy isn't just about what you say—it's also about how well you listen. Active listening involves fully concentrating on the speaker, understanding their message, responding thoughtfully, and remembering the discussion.

By practicing active listening, you show respect and build trust, making others more receptive to your ideas. It also allows you to pick up on subtle cues and underlying issues that might not be immediately apparent.

During a merger process, I was part of a team tasked with integrating departments from two companies. Emotions were high, and many employees were anxious about job security and changes to their roles. In meetings, I focused on listening more than speaking. By acknowledging their concerns and providing honest information when possible, we eased tensions and facilitated a smoother transition.

The Chad Factor—When Diplomacy Is Overlooked

Now, let's revisit Chad. Chad was excellent at making connections and had a knack for being in the right place at the right time. However, his approach sometimes lacked the finesse that diplomacy requires.

On one occasion, Chad was leading a project that required collaboration across multiple departments. Confident in his charm, he assumed everyone would be on board with his ideas. Instead of seeking input, he unilaterally made decisions and presented them as done deals. This approach didn't sit well with other team members who felt bypassed and undervalued.

As a result, cooperation dwindled, and the project stalled. Chad learned the hard way that charisma isn't a substitute for diplomacy. Building consensus and respecting others' expertise are essential for successful collaboration.

Building a Diplomatic Reputation

Being known as a diplomatic professional can enhance your credibility and open doors to new opportunities. People are more likely to trust and seek out individuals who handle situations tactfully and respectfully.

To build this reputation:

- **Practice Self-Awareness:** Understand your own emotions and triggers. This helps you remain composed under pressure.
- **Cultivate Empathy:** Try to see situations from others' perspectives. This understanding can inform your approach and make your interactions more effective.

- **Communicate Clearly and Respectfully:** Choose your words carefully, especially in sensitive situations. Avoid language that could be misinterpreted or cause unnecessary offense.

- **Maintain Professionalism:** Even when disagreements arise, keep interactions professional. This sets a positive example and encourages others to respond in kind.

The Long-Term Benefits of Diplomacy

Diplomacy isn't just about resolving immediate issues; it's an investment in your long-term career. Diplomatic individuals are often seen as leaders, even if they don't hold formal leadership positions. They are the ones who can navigate complex situations, bring people together, and drive projects forward.

Moreover, diplomacy can enhance your upward and downward networks. Superiors appreciate employees who can manage challenges without escalating conflicts, while peers and subordinates value colleagues who respect their contributions and foster a collaborative environment.

Final Thoughts: Making Diplomacy a Habit

Mastering diplomacy is a continuous journey. It requires conscious effort, reflection, and a willingness to learn from each interaction.

But the rewards are significant—improved relationships, enhanced influence, and a more fulfilling professional life.

So, the next time you face a challenging conversation or a complex team dynamic, remember the power of diplomacy. Approach the situation with empathy, listen actively, and communicate thoughtfully. In doing so, you'll not only navigate the immediate challenge but also strengthen the foundation for future success.

The Takeaway

Diplomacy is the art of navigating professional relationships with tact and finesse. It's about influencing outcomes through understanding, empathy, and strategic communication rather than authority or force. By mastering diplomacy, you can build stronger alliances, resolve conflicts effectively, and enhance your reputation as a trusted and respected professional.

Remember, diplomacy isn't about avoiding difficult conversations or suppressing your ideas. It's about engaging with others in a way that respects their perspectives while clearly articulating your own. It's a skill that, once developed, can significantly amplify your impact and accelerate your career growth.

Action Plan: Navigating Office Diplomacy

Objective: Navigate workplace dynamics gracefully to build influence, manage conflicts, and foster alliances without compromising integrity.

Framework: Diplomacy in the workplace requires understanding power dynamics, choosing battles wisely, aligning goals with stakeholders, and fostering trust-based relationships. These steps will help you influence outcomes while fostering a collaborative work environment.

1. Understand and Respect Power Dynamics

Recognizing who holds influence within your organization is critical for success. Engaging the right people ensures your ideas gain traction and align with existing dynamics.

Example: Identify influential players and their roles within your projects. Engage with those who have insight and sway early on, ensuring they're aligned with your vision and invested in the outcome.

2. Choose Your Battles Wisely

Prioritizing which issues to pursue helps maintain momentum and preserves working relationships. Focus on advancing key objectives rather than winning every disagreement.

Example: Before standing firm, ask yourself if the issue is critical to the project's success. When possible, aim for a compromise that honors both perspectives and maintains progress.

3. Gather Support Before Key Meetings

Engaging stakeholders individually ensures their concerns are addressed before collective discussions, reducing the risk of conflict and streamlining decision-making.

Example: Engage with stakeholders individually to address concerns and gather feedback. This proactive approach helps secure agreement and minimizes objections when it matters most.

4. Focus on Issues, Not Personalities

Keeping discussions centered on objectives rather than emotions ensures conflicts remain productive and resolution-focused.

Example: When facing conflict, steer the discussion toward shared objectives. By keeping the focus on project needs, you can reduce personal friction and encourage productive problem-solving.

5. Build Strategic Alliances Beyond Your Team

Fostering relationships across teams builds a support network that can provide valuable insights and assistance when navigating complex challenges.

Example: Invest time in building relationships across teams. Small interactions, like grabbing coffee or offering assistance, can create valuable alliances that support your long-term goals.

Reflection and Self-Monitoring

Weekly Reflection: "Did I navigate power dynamics effectively this week to align key stakeholders and influence outcomes? What worked well, and what could I improve?"

Monthly Reflection: "How have my efforts to build alliances and manage conflicts strengthened my ability to navigate office diplomacy? What additional steps can I take to enhance collaboration and trust?"

Chapter 23

The Importance of Celebrating Wins—Big and Small

It's easy to get caught up in the hustle and bustle of daily work life. We're constantly pushing towards the next deadline, the next project, or the next big goal. But in the rush to achieve more, we often forget to celebrate what we've already accomplished. It's like climbing a mountain and never pausing to enjoy the view—you're missing out on half the journey.

For years, I didn't believe in celebrating small wins. I thought, "Why celebrate until you've reached the top?" It felt like pausing to pat myself on the back would only slow me down. But over time, I realized that waiting for the "big" achievements meant I rarely took a moment to appreciate my progress. And when the big milestones took longer to achieve than I'd planned, I found myself feeling more frustrated than fulfilled.

The Power of Small Wins

Here's the thing: small wins matter. They build momentum, boost morale, and give you the energy to keep going when the road ahead seems long. It's like playing a video game where every little victory gives you that extra boost of energy or unlocks a new level. Without those small victories, the game becomes pretty exhausting.

I've learned that celebrating wins—no matter how small—doesn't mean you're satisfied with where you are. It means you're acknowledging the progress you've made. It's the equivalent of telling yourself, "Hey, you're doing a great job. Keep going." And honestly, we could all use a little more of that encouragement.

Think about it: when was the last time you celebrated a small achievement at work? Maybe you finished that report a day early, or you got a positive email from a client. Did you take a moment to appreciate it, or did you immediately jump to the next task? When you celebrate these small wins, you're not just boosting your own morale—you're creating a culture where progress is valued and recognized.

Creating a Culture of Celebration in Your Team

This isn't just about celebrating your own wins; it's about fostering a culture where your team feels appreciated, too. When I moved into a leadership role, I noticed that my team was working hard, hitting targets, and yet, they seemed exhausted. There was this unspoken mentality that only the big wins mattered—landing a new client, hitting the quarterly target, or delivering a major project. Everything else was just part of the grind.

So, I made a change. We started having a quick "win of the week" session at our Friday meetings. It didn't have to be anything monumental—just something that each person felt good about achieving that week. At first, I thought it might feel forced, but to my surprise, the team got into it. People started sharing things like, "I finally figured out that tricky report formula" or "I had a great conversation with a client today."

Over time, it grew into something more. It wasn't just about work wins anymore—team members started sharing small victories from their personal lives too. One guy shared how his long-time crush said yes to his proposal, and that moment became the highlight of a difficult week for most of us. It turned out that celebrating small wins wasn't just about recognizing progress; it was also about building camaraderie within the team. Those little celebrations brought us closer, made us more than just colleagues, and turned a tough week into one where we still felt connected.

Chad's Unexpected Approach to Celebrations

Even Chad, with all his quirks, had his own way of celebrating progress. He had this ability to find something to celebrate, even when most of us were just trying to survive the workweek. I used to think it was just part of his laid-back nature, but I realized later that he was onto something.

There was this one time when we'd just finished a particularly rough quarter. We didn't hit all our targets, and most of us were ready to write it off as a loss. But instead of dwelling on what went wrong, Chad suggested a quick after-work get-together. "Hey, we've got to recharge for the next round, right? Let's celebrate getting through it," he said with a grin.

It wasn't about pretending that we didn't have more work to do—it was about acknowledging that we'd pushed through a tough time together. It wasn't a grand gesture, but it made a difference. We spent the evening unwinding, sharing stories (both work-related and not), and ended up feeling a lot lighter. The next day, we all came back to work with a bit more energy and perspective.

It's one of the rare times I'll give Chad full credit: he understood that celebrating progress doesn't mean you're satisfied with where you are—it means you're motivated to keep going.

Why Celebrating Wins Matters for Leadership

As a leader, it's easy to focus only on the metrics, the outcomes, and the bottom line. But if you don't take the time to recognize the journey along the way, you risk burning out your team—and yourself. It's not about giving out participation trophies; it's about creating a sense of progress and momentum.

Celebrating wins, both big and small, helps to build a culture where people feel valued. It reminds your team that their efforts matter, even if the end goal is still a work in progress. And let's be real—people work harder and are more committed when they feel seen and appreciated.

It doesn't have to be anything elaborate. A quick shoutout in a meeting, a thank-you email, or even just taking a moment to acknowledge someone's effort can go a long way. Sometimes, I'd send a goofy meme or a GIF to a team member who did a great job—just to remind them that their work didn't go unnoticed. It might seem trivial, but those little gestures can make a world of difference in keeping morale high.

Balancing Celebrations with Accountability

Now, let's be clear: celebrating wins doesn't mean ignoring areas where improvement is needed. It's about balancing positivity with accountability. When you create an environment where wins are celebrated, it becomes easier to address setbacks because the team knows their efforts are valued. It's like building up goodwill in a bank account—you can draw from it when you need to push a little harder or when things don't go as planned.

It's also a way of reminding yourself that progress isn't always linear. You might have weeks where everything goes smoothly, and others where it feels like you're rolling a boulder uphill. Celebrating those little wins can help keep you focused on the bigger picture, even when the day-to-day is challenging.

Turning Wins into Future Motivation

One of the best things about celebrating wins is that it creates a sense of forward momentum. It's like reaching a checkpoint in a video game—it gives you that extra boost to keep moving. And when you're in a leadership role, that sense of momentum can be contagious. A team that feels like it's making progress, even in small ways, is more likely to stay motivated and push through the tougher times.

I've learned that celebrating wins isn't just about looking back; it's about using those moments to fuel the next stage of the journey. When you recognize the progress you've made, you're reminded of what you're capable of achieving. It's like planting a flag on a hill before you climb the next mountain.

So, next time you wrap up a project, hit a milestone, or even just make it through a challenging week, take a moment to celebrate. Grab a coffee, high-five a colleague (even if it's virtual), or just take a breath and appreciate the journey. You've earned it—and it'll give you the energy to keep climbing.

The Takeaway

In the race to meet deadlines and tackle new challenges, it's easy to forget the importance of celebration. But success, whether monumental or minor, deserves recognition. Taking the time to celebrate wins—both big and small—reinforces positive behaviors, boosts morale, and reminds everyone of the progress being made.

Celebrating isn't just for the moment; it's an investment in the future. Each win is a stepping stone that fuels the journey ahead. By recognizing achievements, you're building a culture of appreciation, where people feel valued and motivated to continue pushing forward.

In the end, success isn't a single event but a collection of moments. Recognizing those moments creates momentum. It reminds you that while the journey may be long, it's the accumulation of these wins—each one celebrated—that makes the effort worthwhile.

Action Plan: Building Momentum by Celebrating Progress

Objective: Cultivate a positive environment that values achievements, keeps motivation high, and builds momentum for ongoing progress.

Framework: Celebration is a tool for reinforcing positive behaviors, recognizing effort, and creating a culture where every step forward contributes to long-term success.

1. Recognize Small Wins to Keep Momentum Going

Acknowledging small achievements boosts morale and encourages consistent progress, even when the bigger goals feel distant.

Example: Look for small accomplishments each week, whether it's a task completed early, an efficient meeting, or a helpful client interaction. Acknowledge them informally with a quick "Great work" or a thank-you note to reinforce positive progress without slowing down the pace.

2. Show Appreciation with Thoughtful Gestures

Small gestures of recognition go a long way in creating a positive and motivated team environment.

Example: When someone on your team goes the extra mile, recognize it in a meaningful way. A simple email, a mention in a team chat, or even a casual "thank you" during a conversation can boost morale and let people know their hard work doesn't go unnoticed.

3. Build Celebration into Milestones, Not Just Big Wins

Marking milestones in long-term projects provides a sense of accomplishment and sustains energy for the journey ahead.

Example: Set a few checkpoints during long-term projects. When you hit a milestone, take a moment to appreciate it—whether with a coffee break, a small group acknowledgment, or just a personal reflection. This keeps the team motivated and reinforces a sense of steady progress.

4. Positive Reinforcement with Constructive Feedback

Creating a culture that values progress doesn't mean ignoring areas for improvement. Recognize success while keeping a focus on what's next.

Example: When you celebrate an accomplishment, pair it with a forward-looking conversation about the next steps or areas for refinement. This approach shows appreciation for effort while keeping goals in sight.

5. Use Wins as Fuel for Future Goals

Celebrating progress builds confidence and reinforces a sense of capability, inspiring teams to approach future challenges with renewed energy.

Example: After acknowledging a win, connect it to upcoming goals. Reinforce the impact of the team's work on the bigger picture, using past success as a foundation for future growth.

Reflection and Self-Monitoring

Weekly Reflection: "What small wins did I recognize or celebrate this week? How did this impact team morale and motivation?"

Monthly Reflection: "How have I balanced celebrating progress with maintaining focus on future goals? What can I do to further reinforce a culture of acknowledgment and achievement?"

Chapter 24

Sustaining Career Growth Over Time

When I first started out in my career, I thought success would be like climbing a mountain. I imagined reaching the top, planting my flag, and then enjoying the view. But as it turns out, it's more like running a marathon—one that has no clear finish line. You keep moving forward, sometimes sprinting, sometimes crawling, but the goal isn't just about reaching the next milestone; it's about sustaining your progress over the long haul.

And that's where many people, including myself, get tripped up. We focus so much on the short-term wins—like landing that promotion or acing a project—that we forget to think about what comes next. We forget to ask ourselves, "Where do I want to be in five years? Ten years?" It's a question that's easy to push aside when you're caught up in the day-to-day grind, but it's the key to making sure you're not just running in circles.

The Myth of the "Final Destination"

Early in my career, I had this idea that if I just got that next job title or reached that salary band, I'd finally feel like I'd "made it." In reality, when I got there, I still felt restless. That's when I realized that career growth isn't a destination; it's a journey. And, more importantly, it's a journey that requires continuous effort, learning, and adaptation.

I've always been competitive and ambitious. I rose through the ranks faster than many of my peers, always pushing myself to reach the next level. But there came a point when I took a step back. It wasn't an easy decision—it went against everything I'd been driving towards for years. But I realized that the pace I was moving at wasn't sustainable, at least not if I wanted to keep my sanity intact. My mental and physical health had taken a backseat for too long, and I needed to regain that balance. I wouldn't be sitting here, writing this book, if I hadn't made that decision.

Success means different things to different people, and it means different things to the same person at different points in time. Sometimes, success is climbing the corporate ladder as quickly as possible. Other times, it's about stepping back, reevaluating, and finding a way to thrive without sacrificing your well-being.

Is your path making you happy, or is it keeping you awake at night with anxiety? If it's the latter, then you might not be on the right track. Does your job have you working 12-16 hours a day and traveling four days a week, but you genuinely enjoy the challenges and the people you meet along the way? If that's the case, maybe that's your calling. It's all about finding your own balance.

Thinking Like an Investor

So how do you play the long game? Think of your career like an investment portfolio. You wouldn't put all your money in one stock and hope for the best, right? You'd diversify, keep an eye on market trends, and make adjustments based on where you see future growth. The same principles apply to your career.

Diversification here means building skills outside of your immediate role. For example, if you're a data analyst, don't just focus on getting better at analytics—take some time to understand project management or business strategy. You never know when those skills might come in handy, and they can make you more valuable when new opportunities arise.

A former mentor once told me, "Your career is like a garden. You have to keep planting seeds, even when you don't know when they'll bloom." At the time, it sounded like one of those vague pieces of advice that I'd ignore, but over the years, I've seen the truth in it. It's the side projects, the relationships you build, and the extra skills you pick up along the way that often lead to the most unexpected opportunities. Those are the seeds you plant today that might bloom years down the line.

Staying Relevant in a Changing World

We live in a world where the skills you need today may be obsolete tomorrow. It's both exciting and terrifying. One moment, you're on top of the latest software or management technique, and the next, a new approach is the hot topic at every conference. So, how do you keep up?

Continuous learning is the name of the game. It doesn't mean you have to go back to school or sign up for every certification out there (although those can be helpful). Sometimes, it's as simple as listening to industry podcasts during your commute, reading a new book each month, or attending a webinar on emerging trends. These small steps add up, keeping you sharp and adaptable.

I make it a habit to set aside at least one hour a week for learning. It could be reading articles, watching a tutorial, or just exploring a new tool that I've heard people talk about. And yes, sometimes it feels like just one more thing on the to-do list, but I've found that those little investments in myself pay off in the long run.

Chad's Comfortable Plateau

Chad and I joined the company around the same time, and while our paths diverged, I always kept an eye on what he was up to. Chad

had a natural charm that I lacked, and he used it well. He made connections, built relationships, and he was great at showing up where it mattered most. It paid off too—before long, he found himself in a managerial role, overseeing a team and making decisions that I could only aspire to back then.

For a while, it seemed like Chad had it all figured out. He'd reached a place where he was comfortable, managing a team, earning a solid paycheck, and—most importantly—enjoying the perks that came with his position. He was invited to key meetings, had a direct line to leadership, and even had a reserved spot at the company's golf outings (not that he was any good, but that never seemed to matter).

But as the months turned into years, I started noticing something different about Chad. The fire that he'd had—the drive to learn new things, to adapt to new challenges—wasn't burning quite as brightly anymore. He had found his groove, but he'd also grown a bit too comfortable in it. He stopped attending those industry webinars and brushing up on the latest tools and trends. "Why bother?" he'd joke, "I've got a handle on this."

Then, one year, the company decided to roll out a new, cutting-edge software platform that promised to streamline a lot of the processes Chad's team was managing. It was a big deal—every team had to adapt, learn the new system, and find ways to integrate it into their workflows. Leadership was eager to see which teams could leverage the new platform to its full potential.

Chad, however, resisted. "Why fix what's not broken?" he'd say to anyone who asked. He stuck to the old way of doing things, confident that his established methods would prove more reliable than the untested software. But as weeks turned into months, his team began to fall behind. Other managers embraced the change, finding ways to automate tasks and boost their team's productivity. Chad's team, on the other hand, struggled to keep pace.

It wasn't long before the cracks started to show. While other teams were turning around projects faster, Chad's team lagged behind, still bogged down in the old manual processes. His confidence started to waver. He'd always been the one ahead of the curve, the guy who could talk his way through any challenge. But this time, charm alone couldn't help him. Leadership started noticing the difference, and Chad's reputation as a forward-thinking manager began to take a hit.

Eventually, he had no choice but to dive into the new system, learning it alongside his team. It wasn't easy—especially not with everyone watching him struggle—but to his credit, he managed to turn things around, even if he was a few steps behind the others. But by then, the opportunity to be seen as a leader in the new way of doing things had passed him by.

Chad's story taught me a valuable lesson. It wasn't that he didn't have the skills or the potential—he absolutely did. But he got comfortable, and he underestimated how quickly things could change. It's a reminder that no matter where you are in your career, there's always something new to learn, something you could be better at. And sometimes, that means getting a little uncomfortable, embracing the unknown, and being willing to start from square one again.

Balancing Patience with Ambition

One of the hardest aspects of playing the long game is finding the balance between patience and ambition. It's easy to feel like you're not moving fast enough, especially when you see others around you, like Chad, making leaps in their careers. But here's the thing: slow progress is still progress.

There's a story I love about bamboo. For the first few years, bamboo barely grows above the ground, but then, suddenly, it shoots up at an incredible pace. The reality is that during those "slow" years, it's building a strong root system, preparing for that rapid growth. Sometimes, your career is like that—you're building the foundation, making connections, learning, and growing, even if it doesn't show immediately.

It's okay to want more, to push yourself to grow faster. But remember that the foundations you're building today will support the bigger leaps you want to take tomorrow. It's not a race, and everyone's pace is different.

Comparison is the Thief of Joy

It's tempting to look around at what others are doing, to wonder if you'd be happier or more successful if you'd taken a different path. But comparison is the thief of joy. What matters most is not where you stand relative to others, but whether the path you're on is the right one for you. So ask yourself: Are you building a career that aligns with your values, your goals, and your well-being? If the answer is yes, then keep moving forward. Your journey is uniquely yours, and it's worth embracing every step of the way.

The Takeaway

Playing the long game means understanding that career growth is a marathon, not a sprint. It requires patience, resilience, and adaptability. Long-term success comes from steady progress, with each step building upon the last.

Growth doesn't always happen in a straight line. Setbacks and detours offer opportunities to learn, evolve, and come back stronger. The key is to keep moving forward, even when progress feels slow.

Sustainable career growth balances ambition with well-being and personal fulfillment with career goals. Focusing on the long game creates a path to lasting and meaningful success.

Action Plan: Building Sustainable Career Growth

Objective: Maintain steady progress, stay adaptable, and ensure your career aligns with your long-term goals and personal well-being.

Framework: Sustainable growth is achieved through continuous learning, goal alignment, skill diversification, and balancing ambition with patience to create a fulfilling career.

1. Set Long-Term Goals to Guide Your Path

Without a clear vision, chasing short-term wins can lead to misalignment with your true ambitions. Defining long-term goals ensures every step contributes to a meaningful career journey.

Example: Define where you want to be in five or ten years. Identify key skills, experiences, or roles that align with your vision. Revisit these goals periodically, adjusting them as your priorities evolve to ensure you're building a career that fulfills you over time.

2. Embrace Continuous Learning to Stay Relevant

Industries are constantly evolving, making lifelong learning essential to staying competitive and adaptable.

Example: Dedicate a consistent hour each week to professional growth. Whether it's reading industry news, exploring new tools, or taking a short online course, small, regular investments in learning help keep you sharp and adaptable.

3. Diversify Your Skills to Increase Career Flexibility

Broadening your skillset expands your career options and enables you to contribute more effectively in varied situations.

Example: Identify one skill outside your core responsibilities and set aside time each month to develop it. This could mean learning more about business strategy, improving your communication skills, or gaining familiarity with new software. Over time, these additional skills make you more versatile and valuable.

4. Balance Patience with Strategic Ambition

Career growth often happens incrementally. Trust in steady progress while remaining ambitious about long-term goals.

Example: Break long-term goals into manageable steps, celebrating each small milestone. Remind yourself that growth often happens in stages and that building a strong foundation now sets you up for greater leaps in the future.

5. Stay Grounded by Avoiding Comparisons

Measuring success by comparing yourself to others can lead to frustration. Focus on aligning your path with your values and aspirations.

Example: Reflect on your achievements and values, making sure your goals align with what truly matters to you. Embrace your unique journey and prioritize choices that support both your professional and personal well-being.

Reflection and Self-Monitoring:

Weekly Reflection: "Did I take a meaningful step toward my long-term goals this week? How did I adapt to challenges or changes in my priorities?"

Monthly Reflection: "What progress have I made toward building new skills or diversifying my experience? Are my current efforts aligned with my broader career vision?"

Conclusion – Tying It All Together

We've been through quite the journey together, haven't we? Navigating the twists and turns of corporate life is no small feat, and if there's one thing I hope you've taken away from these pages, it's this: there's no single path to success. The truth is, your career is less like a straight highway and more like a winding road full of detours, scenic routes, and the occasional traffic jam. And that's okay.

Success in the professional world isn't about sticking rigidly to a set plan—it's about adapting, learning, and staying true to what matters most to you. It's about knowing when to push forward and when to step back, when to speak up and when to let others have the floor, and when to focus on the next big goal versus enjoying where you are.

Balancing Ambition and Well-Being

If there's one thing I wish I had understood earlier, it's the importance of balance. Ambition is a powerful thing—it's what drives us to achieve, to push our limits, and to rise to challenges. But left unchecked, it can become all-consuming. The path to success is not about working yourself to the bone, nor is it about coasting along and hoping for the best. It's about finding that sweet spot where you're growing and evolving without losing sight of yourself in the process.

It's also about redefining success as you go. Maybe at one stage, success meant landing a promotion or leading a big project. And maybe now, it means having the time and energy to focus on your family, your hobbies, or, who knows, writing a book of your own. The point is, you get to decide what your goals look like—and you get to change your mind along the way.

And if there's a theme that's run through all these chapters, it's the idea that you don't have to go it alone. Whether it's leveraging your network, finding mentors, or building relationships that matter, the support of others can turn the most daunting challenges into opportunities for growth.

Embracing the Imperfections

In a world that often celebrates the polished highlight reel, it's easy to forget that the real work happens in the messy, in-between moments. It happens when you're figuring out how to communicate a difficult message to your team, or when you're struggling to find balance during a particularly stressful month. It happens when you learn from your mistakes—and when you learn to laugh at them too.

The truth is, success is rarely about perfection. It's about resilience, adaptability, and the courage to keep showing up, even when things don't go according to plan. It's about embracing the grey areas—those moments when the right path isn't clear, but you trust yourself to find a way through.

And along the way, you'll meet people who challenge you, inspire you, and sometimes frustrate you to no end. But each of them brings something valuable to your journey, even if it's not always obvious at first.

Oh, and Before I Forget… About Chad

I know some of you are going to ask me once this book is out—who was Chad, really? Was he my rival, my colleague, or just that guy who seemed to have all the luck while I was working through the tough stuff? Well, here's the truth: there was never just one Chad.

Every Chad in this book was a little different. Sometimes he was that charismatic coworker who had a knack for making connections. Other times, he was the manager who made decisions that left me scratching my head. And sometimes, just sometimes, Chad was me.

You see, it's easy to tell stories where we're the heroes, and the "Chads" of the world are the ones who get in our way. But if I'm being honest, I've had my own Chad moments—times when I coasted, when I took shortcuts, or when I got ahead without necessarily having all the answers. It's a little humbling to admit, but it's also a reminder that none of us are purely the hero or the villain. We're just people, trying to find our way.

Work life, like regular life, is full of shades of grey. It's filled with moments when we get it right, and moments when we don't. And through it all, there's always something to learn—whether it's from the Chads we meet, or from the times when we end up playing that role ourselves.

So, if you take anything from this book, let it be this: Embrace the complexity, stay curious, and remember that there's no single way to get it right. Keep asking questions, keep seeking out the things that make you better, and don't be afraid to laugh at the absurdities along the way. Success isn't about being perfect; it's about finding what works for you and making it your own.

Here's to your journey—wherever it takes you next. And if you run into a few Chads along the way, well, just remember: there's something to learn from them too.

Before You Go… Let's Keep in Touch!

First off, **thank you** for reading *The Lost Map To Your Career*. If something in this book resonated with you—whether it gave you a fresh perspective, helped you navigate a tough situation, or simply made you laugh—I'd love to hear about it.

If this book made a difference in your career, the best way to help others find it is by **leaving a quick review on Amazon**. Your words matter more than you know. Even just a few sentences about what you found helpful can go a long way in making sure this book reaches the people who need it most.

And if you haven't already, **don't forget to grab your free Career FAQs eBook**—a quick-reference guide packed with answers to common career challenges.

You can find it at www.shyamuthaman.com/careerFAQs.

For more resources, updates, and upcoming releases, you can always reach me at www.shyamuthaman.com.

Wishing you all the success in the world—keep learning, keep growing, and most importantly, keep moving forward.

— **Shyam Uthaman**

Made in the USA
Monee, IL
19 May 2025